HOW TO THINK 10 X

Accelerate Positivity. Accomplish
Dreams. Achieve Success.

MANJUL TEWARI

www.manjultewari.com

To My Parents

YOUR FREE GIFT

As a token of my thanks for taking out time to read my book, I would like to offer you a free gift. Download your Free PDF eBook by visiting the link

https://www.manjultewari.com/my-free-e-book/

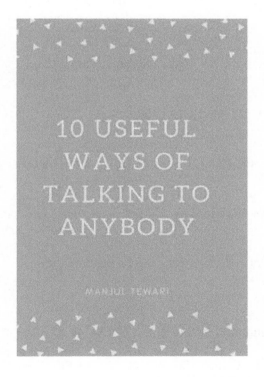

Ten Useful Ways of Talking To Anybody

TABLE OF CONTENTS

CHAPTER 1:
INTRODUCTION

"Life opens up opportunities for you, and you either take them or you stay afraid of taking them." — *Jim Carrey*

He was born in Canada in the 60s in a not-so-privileged family. His mother was in poor health. So, he was always at her bedside, never for a moment leaving her alone. He looked after her and cared for her since he was young. As a child, he would do everything possible to make his mother cheerful. His father worked hard as a clerk in a local CA firm while trying to provide for the family as best as he could manage.

His father had aspired to be a visual artist, but due to financial constraints, he had to give up his dreams as he found them to be impracticable. The family continued to somehow manage until his father lost his job. He tried desperately to find a new one but did not succeed.

Days passed into months. Having survived on their meager savings, ultimately, they had to leave the house as they were not able to afford the rent. They shifted into a worn-out, rickety van. The boy, now a teenager, fully understood the situation they were in, and began working in a steel factory so that he could pitch in a little with his earnings. He stared into his future and had dreams of his own too, but his priorities were with his family.

The boy learned life lessons quite early in his life. He had seen his father give up his aspirations and settle for what he thought was a secure option of getting a job as a clerk, yet he still could not succeed. The boy reasoned that failure or success does not guarantee certainty in whatever you choose to do. He reasoned, *"Why not do something you dream of doing and try to succeed? Even if you fail, you will be comfortable in the thought that at least you attempted your aspirations"*.

He loved to entertain people with his antics. This was his calling. He wanted to be an actor and a stand-up comedian. When he turned 16, his father took him to his first stage performance. This turned out to be a complete failure. No one in the audience expressed any amusement at his presentation. The boy felt utterly let down and disillusioned by his performance. He began to feel that he was not good at it.

But deep down, he knew that he loved what he was doing. He just had to make extra effort for it. So, he practiced in every moment he could spare within his daily routine. He rehearsed, repeating his lines and acting whenever he was in solitude, even when he was taking a shower. At the second show, his performance was much better, and this time the audience loved it and gave a rousing standing ovation. As time flew by, his resolve to be an actor became stronger.

He moved to America to fulfill his dream. He got a few calls for auditions, but getting an assignment to act was still a far cry. However, he did not give up on his dream of becoming a great actor one day. Every night he looked at the Hollywood signboards and imagined that well-known directors would approach him to sign him for a movie, that fans were surrounding him for an autograph. He still had nothing with him except his dreams and dreams alone, which he was not willing to dump and return home.

Months passed and he had a few auditions but got no work. Still, he was hopeful. He held onto his belief that success was not too far away. So one fine day, he took out his checkbook, took a leaf from it, and wrote himself a post-dated $10 million check to himself. He dated it five years in the future. He vowed to himself that he would earn that money before the date on the check. It was as if he was seeking from the Universe what he aspired for so badly.

And the universe responded favorably to his ambition. He became an actor, and after a string of successful roles, a few years later he got a $10 million check for his movie. The movie "Dumb and Dumber" was a big hit globally.

The net worth of the little boy from Canada "Jim Carrey" is over $180 million, and he is rated as one of the most accomplished movie actors in the world.

Says the famous actor, *"You can fail at what you don't want, so you might as well take a chance on doing what you love".*

Jim Carrey was an ordinary child with extraordinary dreams. He thought big. He never doubted himself. His self-doubt could have limited him to remaining a factory worker for his entire life, but he strived hard to make his dreams come true. We too can make it big, provided we are not afraid to take the plunge. Provided we are not afraid of thinking big.

What this book will offer you

The book describes simple and effective ways in which one can practice "Thinking Big" in one's daily life. The book guides you to place complete trust in your conviction and be brave. Some of the topics that have been suitably explained in greater detail in the book are listed below:

- **How to widen your knowledge base** by expanding your network of successful people. Multiply your thinking 10 times. **Think from a longer perspective.** Ready to learn new aspects of life?

- How to have complete **faith in yourself.**

- There is **no substitute for hard work.** Go beyond daydreaming—toil hard to make it happen.

- **Explore the new frontiers of Big Thinking.** Come out of your self-notified comfort level. **Achievers and big thinkers jump into sports** regardless of being given a formal invitation. Accomplished people are self-advocates.

- The **Whys and Whats of Our Big Picture. Define your why before you dive in**

- **Knowing the latest trends is key to your success. Stay flexible with your ideas, but be firm in your vision.** Don't forget the importance of marketing and advertising when thinking big. Understanding the influence of thinking big. **Motivation is taking action daily. Success and big thinking are correlated.**

From this book you will learn how to:

- Have an undivided focus on your goal. Mindset, more than intellect, matters. Stay focused on your vision. Big dreams are to be given due reverence and respect.

- Seek out help and the universe has a way of assisting you. Know your areas of control and limitations.

- Channelize the positive energies of the people around you. An accomplished person knows how to move on from a defeat. Achievers and big thinkers go for the big-ticket experience.

- To take the prudent direction of achievement. Have total faith in yourself. Applying your secret dream from "me to we" to make it a reality.

- Revaluate your strategy and adapt to change as you move forward. Visualize and Assess Your Assets.

- Take the first baby step and, thereafter, take one small step at a time.

The book focuses on the following areas in great detail:

- What is the Magic of Thinking Big and Being Successful?

- How to Become a Big Picture Thinker. Get out of the box and generate creative ideas;

- Setting Goals after due diligence;

- Essential Keys to Drive the Big Thinking Process;

- How Big Thinking Can Lead to Success;

- How Big Picture Thinkers have limitless boundaries.

This book equips its readers with innovative and creative strategies to think big. Since these have been tried and tested by thinkers and philosophers, if they have worked for them, they should work for us. (Yes, I am in the same boat.) I am confident that these will work for you and me as well. Thinking Big is for all those who can think. It is not a realm of the matter solely for a select few. Thinking Big is for anyone who wants to think and act differently. So let us just start the process of thinking big as explained in the book and try to bring innovation into our lives.

Therefore, let's begin to understand the notion better by going through the first chapter and learning the practical steps involved in the process of "Thinking Big".

This book is a road map to knowing and applying how to think big when our brains begin to tell us that it is risky to take up a venture that we always dreamed of. We then begin to put doubts about our capabilities and our potential. Our intellect belittles us by advising that we are not capable of doing what others have accomplished. Let's for a moment think big for a change. Let's keep the intellectual side of our brain to one side. For one day, at least, let's think big. That will enable us to write in our journal what our dreams are and what we aspire for in our life. Let us not bother about other people's opinions or how absurd they may appear. Let us write it down in our diary and work hard to make it possible. Let that jotting in our dairy be a source of a reminder and also a submission to the universe. Let us follow the mantra of **"Think Big, Work Hard, and make our dreams come true"**.

Now in the very first chapter, we will learn about Jack Ma's stupendous growth story of Ali Baba fame. We will also learn to master simple but effective steps towards thinking big and being successful by generating creative and workable ideas that we are passionate about.

CHAPTER 2:
THE MAGIC OF THINKING BIG AND BEING SUCCESSFUL

"We don't want to be number one in China. We want to be number one in the world." — *Jack Ma*

Developing one of the leading global e-commerce companies requires no expert or specific level of knowledge, no brilliance in math, or even a business plan. What does it take, then? Let's take a look at Jack Ma's growth story - one of the wealthiest men in the world, with a net worth of around $43.4 billion.

Born in 1964, Jack Ma had a particular fascination for learning the English language. So when he was just 12 years old, he would ride his bicycle for 40 minutes to reach one of the swanky hotels in his home city, Hangzhou, and patiently wait for foreign tourists to emerge. He offered them a deal that many of the tourists could not refuse. He offered to show them around the city as a travel guide, and in return, the tourists had to teach him how to speak English. He would wait outside the international hotel, in rain or snow, day after day, year after year. A chance meeting with a friendly Australian family led to Ma being invited to Australia.

Although he improved his English considerably, his math remained weak, and he was unable to pass the university-level examination on the first attempt. In 1988, he was able to find himself a job as an English teacher. On a trip to Seattle, his friend told him about the importance of the internet in the times to come. This one exposure to the internet was going to shape his entire destiny. He was so mesmerized by the concept of the internet that in the same year he established a company, China Yellow Pages, which barely remained afloat. His office space consisted of a single room with a table and a chair in the center and a very old PC on top of it. Ma had spent his entire savings establishing his company.

One of the biggest issues faced by Ma was that there was no internet in his hometown, Hangzhou. In such a scenario, nobody would have entertained the idea of establishing an internet company in the first place. But Ma was a little different from the others. Initially, he convinced his friends of the enormous potential of the internet. He even showed a screenshot of a website being developed by his acquaintances in Seattle. Due to his magnificent power of persuasion, he garnered $2,400 from his prospective clients for fees for designing and uploading the home pages of their companies on the internet. A no-mean achievement by any standards.

While remembering his struggle during his initial days, Jack Ma says, "I was treated as a con man for three years".

"We want to be number one in the world."

Mixing his unshakable perseverance level with experimentation, Ma kept adjusting his business model over the next couple of years. In 1990, he set up Alibaba Group as a business-to-business e-commerce platform. Jack Ma later remembered: "The first week, we had seven employees. We would buy and sell ourselves. In the second week, somebody started to sell on our website. We bought everything they sold. We had two rooms full of things we had no use for, all garbage — to tell people that it works".

From the very beginning, Jack Ma set high goals for himself. Just after he founded his company, he told the journalists that: "We want to be number one in the world, not just in China." He had a meeting with his employees in his one-room office to videotape it for posterity. During the filming, he posed a question to himself, "Where will the company be in the next ten years?" He replied to his question by saying, "We do not have any competitors in China, but in Silicon Valley, and we should position Alibaba as an international website".

While trying to raise capital for his company from prospective clients, Ma did not have any plans for them that they normally expected to see in their meetings. Jack Ma thought, "If you plan, you lose. If you don't plan, you win". However, his likely investors initially could not see Ma's principle. However, due to his charismatic manners, he managed to get Goldman Sachs to invest $5 million in his company.

Jack Ma's example shows that entrepreneurial instinct, or perception, and being open to new knowledge are much more essential than the formal book knowledge that is offered in management schools the world over. Ma once said in a lecture, "It is often vital to unlearn what has been taught in business schools". Only then will the MBA graduates be of some use. Business schools teach knowledge, but what is required for running a successful enterprise is wisdom, which comes from experience. Knowledge can be gained through hard work.

"I'm Not Good at Technology."

Ma said he was not good at technology. He was trained to be a school teacher, yet he started as an internet entrepreneur, ultimately achieving success in running China's largest e-commerce enterprise. Ma said all he knew about computers was how to browse and send and receive e-mails. After establishing his e-commerce business, Ma then went on to set up Taobao, the largest Chinese business-to-consumer shopping website, ultimately elbowing his competitor e-Bay China in 2007, which was a bigger company than Ma's. He went on to set up Alipay in 2004, the world's largest internet payment service. Ma was, from day one, open to big, innovative ideas. He believes that all entrepreneurs should be ready to face adversaries at all times and **"never give up"**.

We draw a string of lessons from Jack Ma's life and his entrepreneurial skills. Thinking big and having deep and complete faith in your dreams is one of many beliefs of the master entrepreneur. "As long as you're going to be thinking anyway, think big," says a famous quote by Donald John Trump, the American politician, media personality, and businessman who served as the 45th president of the United States from 2017 to 2021. Irrespective of whether you like Trump or not, it is a fact that when you start thinking big, you start to pull big things into your life. One of the most highlighted points of difference between successful and unsuccessful people is their way of thinking. Successful people constantly opt to think big, dream big, and imagine themselves contributing to it. Besides, success is achieved not by the size of one's brain or IQ as much as it is by the quantum of one's thinking. If given the option, most people would prefer to join and work for Amazon rather than a small unknown company. The reason is that the majority of large corporations have lofty goals and aspirations. That works as a natural pull for people. In any case, spectators generally prefer to go to watch the final match instead of the qualifying round matches.

The world around you is not interested in your playing small. You fail to enthuse people around you, and they feel apprehensive when you minimize your aspirations and your dreams. Thinking big heralds big results when you begin to take concrete actions based on sound judgment. Keeping in view life's short duration, you might as well make it big if you decide to make it. But because some people are so attuned to thinking small, either they tried and failed, or their close ones told them not to take risks and be practical. This process of thinking small begins at a young, impressionable age when a child asks a seemingly silly question in a classroom and gets laughed at. Or your parents or friends tell you, you cannot do this or that. It is pertinent to remember that one of the greatest human weaknesses is to think of oneself as low. Targeting low after believing that I am not good enough. Remember, high-paying jobs have fewer applications as people feel they are not the right candidate for the job. Hence, keep reminding yourself that you are much better than you think you are. As you are the master of your thinking process, you can select the option of thinking big or thinking small. You can very well decide what you plan to do with your life.

Ways of enhancing our mindset to think big

(a) Imagine the options

As you start to think in your mind, you might as well think big. Imagine all the good that can happen to you as you start to think big. With an affirmative, positive, and helpful approach, a person having an IQ level of 100 is likely to acquire more wealth than a person who is uncooperative, negative, and unhelpful, having an IQ level of 120. You should not let the fear of success or failure stop you from achieving what you imagine and dream of. Imagine that the possibilities are just endless. Napoleon Hill said in his book, Think and Grow Rich, **"Whatever the mind can conceive and believe, it can achieve".**

Albert Einstein, the great scientist who gave the theory of General Relativity and was awarded a Nobel Prize, said, "Imagination is more vital than knowledge". Logic will get you from A to B, but imagination will take you everywhere. "Imagination or thinking that guides you is of greater importance than the knowledge that you may have."

The creator of Disney World, Walt Disney, was fired by his newspaper for lacking creativity in 1919. Walt Disney continued with his imagination and created Mickey Mouse and Disneyland, and the rest, as they say, is history.

Never stop thinking about all the great possibilities that can happen to you and your life. As you invest in thinking big, so will you notice an increase in the same proportion in the amount of your mental happiness and general satisfaction, and even an increase in your bank balance.

(b) Reading increases your perception

If you read more, you can change yourself into a big thinker. Yet another way to expand your thinking horizons. Knowledge comes by reading about it, hearing about it, and visiting the area yourself. So do not let a lack of knowledge limit you in any way. Be a voracious reader. It is one of the simplest ways to expand your knowledge horizons. As you read more and more, you begin to realize how much more information and knowledge is yet to be acquired.

(c) Widen your knowledge base by expanding your network of successful people

By expanding the network of successful people, you can also increase your knowledge base, just as you do by reading more books on relevant topics. There is so much to learn from those who have accomplished something in their sphere of activity. Learning from such people is a powerful tool. Observing or reading about such successful people will help us learn about their paths to success, how they overcame challenges and obstacles, and how to pursue their advice and suggestions for realizing your dreams.

One visit to a billionaire friend's house can teach you an array of intellectually enriching experiences by learning about the person and their accomplishments. While you are comfortable in your thoughts that you have $1 million stashed in your bank account, a visit to the house of your billionaire friend reveals that one of the cars in his fleet alone costs many times more. Hence, when you talk to people who have made it big in their lives, your thinking prowess also increases.

You are further encouraged to think higher and higher by pushing the limits further.

(d) Multiply your thinking 10x

Thinking big requires multiplying it at least ten times. e.g., increase your career goal by ten times. The successes that you envisage in your life should be multiplied ten times. Never think small. Have big dreams. If you think big, you will reap big. If you think small, you will reap small. You will harvest whatever you have seen in that measure. If you do not think big, you live small, limited by your thinking that you cannot make it big. Hence, when you dream big and put in some tangible action, you begin to reap the benefits, unlike the majority of others who play safe and, thereby, small, see themselves as capable of attaining small goals only. Precisely for this reason, you must increase your goals by ten times.

This, by no measure, means you will have to work ten times more to achieve your target. It means that when you raise the bar of your life's goals, you have to adopt an altogether different approach, and an altogether different strategy as you may have to think creatively and "out of the box" to achieve your goal. For example, you will have to adopt a different strategy for landing a job that gets you $10,000 a month, than for a job that will fetch you $100,000 a year. Earnestly, believe in whatever goal you want to set up, on the road to progress without you dragging your feet on the target. Besides, it is said that if the goals that you have set for yourself do not frighten you, you are probably not setting them high enough.

Think of success and you will succeed. Think of failure and you will fail. You will reap whatever you have sown. Always be enthused with positivity. Remove all negativity from your life. Your life's motto should be to embrace positive energy. Phrases such as "impossible" or "cannot be done" should not be in one's vocabulary. As such thoughts close the door to fresh opportunities and success. Where there is a will, there is a way.

(e) Do away with all your constraints.

Thinking big requires you to get rid of all your constraints and inadequacies. Stop thinking about all the restrictions that prevent you from achieving big things in life. Such as you may think, you do not have time for it, you do not have money to fulfill your goal, or you are not fully qualified to do the job. Such thoughts act like iron chains that pull you away from completing your goal.

The goals that you are setting for yourself are for the future, whereas you are comparing your present situation. The fact remains that the future may look brighter if you try hard enough and the present circumstances may not be prevalent in the future. A person of modest means can also achieve success if they are clear about their goals. Hence, think of these limitations as only temporary and transient. You have to look beyond these restrictions and set yourself on the road to success. For instance, ask yourself a question as to what you are going to do if you have $100 million. This way, you have set aside all the restrictions and mental limitations and have started to think big. What goals are you going to pursue if you have both time and money with you? By removing the fetters of restrictive thinking, you start to visualize big. Hence, by looking at things as they should be and not as they are, one frees oneself from all the restrictive thinking that is holding you down to your present. For instance, a salesperson sees every customer, big or small, as a potential future customer who may be instrumental in ushering in higher sales in the upcoming months.

(f) Think in the long perspective

There is a general habit of people thinking about their near future and not thinking from a long-term perspective. Thinking in short measures limits you from achieving your full potential. Bill Gates, one of the richest men in the world, once said, "Most people overestimate what they can do in one year and underestimate what they can do in ten years". Success is never achieved in a short time. You have to think for a long time to achieve success. All big businesses at the time of their start were small businesses. By taking baby steps and thereby taking up a series of steps in the right direction, you set yourself on the road to success. When you start to think from a longer perspective, you also gradually venture out of your comfort zone.

(g) Ready to learn new aspects of life?

Be ever ready to try and experiment with new aspects of life, as the example of Jack Ma shows. Try reading new books, making new acquaintances, trying out new eateries, watching new movies and new live dramas in theatres, experimenting with a new diet; trying out a new route to work or home, thinking positively, smiling often, being happy, and laughing a lot.

Mark Twain once said, "Twenty years from now, you will be more disappointed by the things that you didn't do than by the ones you did". So throw off the bowlines. Sail away from the safe harbor. Catch the trade winds in your sails. Explore. Dream. Discover." As wisely said in the quote, lift anchors and be ready to sail to unknown and uncharted courses and territories, away from your safe limits, without the fear of failing. Do not belittle your latent potential by thinking small and dreaming small. Try it once, and you will then realize your true potential.

Completely ignore the people who say it cannot be done, or it's impossible, or no one has ever done it before. Because if you try and succeed, you will be the first one to achieve the feat. Do not be ignorant of what you can achieve. You will never know your actual potential unless and until you do it. Big success only comes when you start to think big. At the same time, stay at arm's length and completely ignore people with a negative outlook and with negative vibes who may be your friends, relatives, or colleagues. You have to manage your environment in such a manner that you are surrounded by people with positive energy. Continued association with negative people who are, in most probability, unsuccessful, mediocre people themselves, can transform you into a negative thinker as well. Be vigilant to identify such people early and maintain a safe distance.

(h) Have complete faith in yourself

You need to find what is best suited for you to achieve in life, what also makes you happy, and then pursue it relentlessly, even if it may appear strange to others. Remember, you have only a limited time at hand. Before you decide to settle down while going with the flowing current, you need to turn that dream of yours into a reality by giving everything you have got and also by firmly believing and placing **complete trust in your dreams.**

(i) Do it differently

When you choose your way to success, you do it by following your method instead of copying or following others. You have complete faith in traveling along the adopted path even though it has not been traveled before by anyone. You may be a pioneer and the first one to have tried the path that you have adopted. Be a leader and give 100 percent to your cherished goal. By thinking outside of the box, you may be the new pathfinder and the setter of a new record. Never be scared to follow your conscience and nurture a dream. You can achieve outstanding results only if you are not afraid of trending on pathways that have not been ventured into before. Discard the safety of the shore and sail out into open waters if you desire to seek out new, undiscovered frontiers.

(j) Fail forward and fail fast

Disappointments and letdowns are part of our lives. We should accept them with open arms. They teach us vital lessons for us to take care of in the future. Hence, to achieve our end goals, we should be fully geared up to take the decision. Even if we do not succeed initially, having learned our lessons and being unmindful of our fall, we should be adaptive in our approach and stand up again to dash our pre-set goal. You may have to court peril and pitfalls, without which you cannot achieve your 100 percent. You cannot push yourself to the next level hard enough if you don't learn from your mistakes and plan your next move accordingly.

To fail is part of the journey towards the achievement of our goal. Failure is a master who makes you wiser by making you aware of many unknown things. And when you gain knowledge in such a way, you become strengthened afterward. You are even more determined in your efforts and your resolve not to give up. Your path to success is hence charted out accordingly.

(k) No point in listening to a cynic

It is best to listen to your inner voice when it comes to achieving your cherished goal and remain clear of all pessimists. They may try to wean you off from your goal in life by laying stress on you regarding all that may go wrong (both imaginary or based on hearsay) in your journey. Since you only know about your strengths and your vision and mission in life, you are your best judge. So listen to your inner voice each and every time you are in doubt.

It is not possible to make everyone happy. You are the master of your destiny. Hence, you are free to choose your path. Avoid advice from those who may doubt your abilities and capacity to achieve your exquisite goal. At best, ponder over it, see for yourself what is best suited for you, and make your own decision. Do not allow yourself to be dragged down by all the pessimism and disapproval of your peers. You are the best judge to decide if there is any element of truth in the opinion of the people around you. Once you have decided what is best suited for you, do not let the negative vibes of such people obstruct your progress toward your goal. Ignoring and staying clear of such unwarranted negative advice will ensure that you remain focused and committed.

(l) There is no substitute for hard work

Whatever path you choose, it gives you your full potential. The lackadaisical approach does not work at all. Give everything that you have to achieve the goal you have set for yourself. Shortcuts in life do not pay off.

Success does not come cheaply. You have to pay for it. Be willing to pay for it. You can hope to go that extra mile only if you put in the extra effort that is required for it. If you are not willing to work hard, then stop aspiring to have a good life. To get results and make a difference, you have to find time and consistently work towards it.

(m) Give back to society

Give back to society by way of helping others in some form or another. The more you contribute to society at large, the more your own life will be enriched, both spiritually and materialistically, in greater measure. Just go on and try it at least once. It is considered one of the greatest rewards for doing service to humanity. If you extend a helping hand to the needy and vulnerable sections of society, your own life will be further enriched and fulfilled. That is how the law of the universe works.

(n) The bottom line

Enthusiastically accept more challenges and opportunities. Your mind will embrace more of them as they come, as capacity is only a state of mind. Remember, top-level people do a lot more, and so can you. So trust yourself. Whether you succeed in life or not will largely depend on your continued ability to think big. Breaking some rules while not being afraid to fail and not heeding the opinion of all the people who have a negative approach, being an unswerving hard worker, and giving back to society in some form or another should see us sail through the path to success and growth. Playing it safe and dreaming small will not bring in big success.

Steve Jobs, widely considered a visionary and a genius, oversaw the launch of such revolutionary products as the iPod and the iPhone, said once, "Start small, think big. Don't worry about too many things at once. Take a handful of simple things, to begin with, and then progress to more complex ones. Think about not just tomorrow, but the future. Put a ding in the universe".

Here we come to the end of this chapter. In the next chapter, we will discuss ways to become a creative big-picture thinker by "thinking out of the box".

Actionable Takeaways

(a) Imagine the options

As you start to think in your mind, you might as well think big. Imagine all the good that can happen to you as you start to think big. You should not let the fear of success or failure stop you from achieving what you imagine and dream of. Imagine that the possibilities are just endless.

(b) Reading increases your perception

If you read more, you can change yourself into a big thinker. Knowledge comes by reading about it, hearing about it, and visiting the area yourself. So do not let a lack of knowledge limit you in any way. Be a voracious reader.

(c) Widen your knowledge base by expanding your network of successful people

By expanding the network of successful people, you can also increase your knowledge base, just as you do by reading more books on relevant topics. There is so much to learn from those who have accomplished something in their sphere of activity. Learning from such people is a powerful tool. Observing or reading about such successful people will help us learn about their paths to success, how they overcame challenges and obstacles, and how to pursue their advice and suggestions for realizing your dreams.

(d) Multiply your thinking 10 times

Thinking big requires multiplying it by at least ten times. e.g., increase your career goal by ten times. The successes that you envisage in your life should be multiplied ten times. Never think small. Have big dreams. If you think big, you will reap big. It is said that if the goals that you have set for yourself do not frighten you, you are probably not setting them high enough.

(e) Do away with all your constraints

Get rid of all your constraints and inadequacies. Stop thinking about all these restrictions that prevent you from achieving great things in life. Such thoughts act like iron chains that pull you from completing your goal.

(f) Think in a longer perspective

Success is never achieved in a short time. You have to think for a long time to achieve success.

(g) Ready to learn new aspects of life?

Try reading new books; making new acquaintances, trying out new eateries; watching new movies and new live dramas in theatres; experimenting with finding a new route to get to work or home, being upbeat, grinning frequently, and having a good time. Explore. Dream. Discover.

(h) Trust yourself completely

Turn that dream of yours into reality by giving everything you have got and also firmly believing and placing complete trust in your dreams.

(i) Do it differently

When you choose your way to success, you do it by following your method instead of copying or following others. Be a leader and give 100 percent to your cherished goal. Never be scared to follow your conscience and nurture a dream.

(j) Fail forward and fail fast

Disappointments and letdowns are part of our lives. We should accept them with open arms. They teach us vital lessons for us to take care of in the future. Hence, to achieve our end goals, we should be fully geared up to take a decision. Even if we do not succeed initially, having learned our lessons and being unmindful of our fall, we should be adaptive in our approach, and stand up again to dash our pre-set goal.

Initially, you may feel uneasiness, distress, or anxiety as you topple and tumble. At first, the outcome could be disheartening.

But these efforts and experiments will yield certain key learnings that will help in sharpening your skills. Gradually, your perseverance and consistent effort daily will propel you to your desired goals. You will begin to notice the improvement in results in due course. It will be largely due to your continued practice and incorporation of feedback. Hence, thinking big, coupled with experimentation, will lead to the actualization of your goals, making them a reality.

(k) No point in listening to a cynic

It is best to listen to your inner voice when it comes to achieving your cherished goal and remain clear of all pessimists. So listen to your inner voice every time you are in doubt.

(l) There is no substitute for hard work

Whatever path you choose, it gives you your full potential. The lackadaisical approach does not work at all. Give everything that you have to achieve the goal you have set for yourself. Shortcuts in life do not pay off. Success does not come cheaply.

(m) Give back to society

Give back to society by way of helping others in some form or the other. The more you contribute to society at large, the more your own life will be enriched, both spiritually and materialistically, in greater measure.

(n) The bottom line

Enthusiastically accept more challenges and opportunities. Your mind will embrace more of it as they come, as capacity is only a state of mind. Remember, top-level people do a lot more, so can you! So trust yourself.

CHAPTER 3:
BECOME A BIG PICTURE THINKER. GET OUT OF THE BOX AND GENERATE CREATIVE IDEA

"Believe Big. The size of your success is determined by the size of your belief. Think little goals and expect little achievements." — David J. Schwartz

A young boy of 12 years was fondly gazing at an attractive car. He spoke to its owner, who was standing beside it, "That's a great car. It must be expensive."

"Yes," the man proudly replied, "my brother gifted it to me."

The boy says, "Oh," before pausing to think.

"What are you thinking, young man?" the man asked the boy. "Let me guess. You are thinking about how you can also have a car like this."

"No. No," the boy replied, "I want to become like your brother."

Just like the young boy, we have to start thinking big. Here we will be discussing how to adopt certain strategies for becoming a big-picture thinker. There are times when you are at a loss to perform seemingly easy tasks when they become hard to carry out. You begin to feel that, "I am the only one affected by the problem and no one else." You become disappointed and annoyed, while not being able to do this easy-to-perform task. "For instance, when my art teacher in primary school asked me to draw with watercolors, she ensured that I outlined with a pencil first. She told me, "Draw an apple first with a pencil before filling it with watercolor." That's a normal and easy task, and most artists take to drawing a pencil sketch before filling it in watercolor, but it was hard for me to draw as I had not practiced it often. Similarly, during a weekly departmental meeting, the head of the department asked everyone to give new and creative suggestions to increase production and sales. Well, it was easier said than done. You need planning and preparation to come out with flying colors in giving creative and innovative ideas while dreaming big.

Let's start with the first thing first. Why think big?

First of all, there is a need to know how to think big. We have to start by thinking beyond our routine and think of something unique. Here, the box referred to is not the same as our mind, as it is not possible to think out of our mind. The box is then a defined limit within our minds. The box is an imaginary limit between what we know so far and what we have not given a thought to. We are quite familiar with living within the four contour walls of a box. A question that naturally comes to our mind is that when we live comfortably inside our known limits, why should we risk our prestige by going beyond our safe perimeter and searching for new ideas? We have, after all, worked 24-7 developing our status and prestige, so why should we put it at stake? Why should we risk stepping outside our known limits at all? Is stepping out can be treated as some sort of lavishness or opulence, or is it a sheer need and requirement? Let us understand it further.

There is, after all, no comfort in stepping out. It is a basic necessity for all thinking human beings. Why is thinking big a basic necessity for all of us? Because we, as individual human beings living today, are part of a well-defined network in society. Individually, we are small joints or segments in the entire network. We contribute and share ideas on a real-time basis. We, as individual beings, have the same data, and if we do not generate new ideas, if we do not think afresh, then all of us are left with the same old idea. And that is a terrible thing to have. Hence, it is not a luxury but a necessity to step out of our known limits and generate new and evolving ideas to earn our solemnity as thinking human beings. It makes a big difference to us, as an individual, if we generate and share new ideas with the entire knowledge chain. Hence, to think creatively and offer new ideas is not an extravagance at all. It is an absolute must for us as thinking individuals.

Let us understand what the knowledge chain is within our minds. When a child is born, it starts with a preliminary inherited legacy. Then gradually, our boundaries of knowledge begin to expand as we first learn from our parents and others closely related to us, and then from the experiences of our teachers in our centers of learning. This learning experience is indirect as our teachers teach us about their experiences and the discoveries and creations of other individuals.

Then comes our own direct experience, our achievements, and our disappointments that complete us as we are. The limits of our own experiences (or our box) continue to be expanded, and we are quite comfortable staying within that periphery set by our own experience (or box). Whatever we think within the limits, we feel quite safe and secure. Outside the limits, things are not clear and they feel it is risky to venture out of the box. But when it comes to building up and protecting our dignity, we must venture out of this box. How do we simply do that? Do we have to wait for an apple to fall on our heads to start venturing out of the box? Or are there some well-defined and clear-cut methods? Within the boundaries of our direct knowledge and experience, we have ideas, lots of them, and when we think about a focused area, we also know how things should be. So we know about the requirements, about specifications, and about how things are as they always have been. But if we go outside the box, we need to spice it up with more flavor, which could be silly and absurd, and something that could not seem relevant either.

This is what is known as divergent information that we need to cross the borders within our minds, from what we know so far and what we do not know where to go once we are out of the box, as there is no preset path. That is the mental frame of our mind when we venture out of the periphery of our direct knowledge or our box. Sometimes the fear of venturing into unknown territory compels us to immediately return to our box which we consider a safe place. However, this is an enticement that we must defy. We must appreciate the need for long thinking. The concept of long-term thinking is different from brilliant thinking, fast thinking, deep thinking, etc. So what is thinking? It is some engaging thought that takes us far. For example, when listening to music, we do not judge a single musical note; we, on the other hand, listen to the entire song.

Similarly, with our ideas, we need to go far where they have never been applied before. While venturing out of the box, we can use the association of ideas, a combination of ideas, the extraction of principles, and the application of these principles to areas and concepts where they have never been validated before. While validating such concepts and ideas, we need to be open-minded and look for alternatives, not for correct answers. Because when you creatively think outside of the box, there is no single correct answer or path. There could be many possible alternatives or paths.

And just in case we are fortunate, we may find ourselves with a new idea in our journey of exploring outside of the box. Though the value of the new idea or concept could be enormous, we may not see its real importance as it has never been experienced before. We also let ourselves down, belittling ourselves as the inventors of the new idea. "Who am I to be the generator of that new idea? Perhaps someone had already thought about it earlier. If this concept is correct, then someone must have thought about it earlier." We have to defy such notions as such thoughts can destroy our ideas and concepts. We have to think in terms of this new concept of solving another problem that may not be entirely yours. Serendipity may happen. All it requires is the eye to observe it from the right perspective to see how it makes a difference. It is even more understandable when we view it from the perspective of our environment. Man is a social animal and has evolved ever since the Stone Age. To usher in something new to the environment, man must bring in new ideas by thinking outside of the box.

What conditions are conducive to thinking outside the box?

It is generally felt that the conditions that are most favorable for men to think outside of the box are those in which men are encouraged to think creatively. When people are assured that while their creative ideas may or may not work, they will not be penalized or reprimanded for committing mistakes involuntarily. Then they are encouraged to come out of their comfort zones and begin to think outside of the box. If you want to kindle and inspire people to come out of their comfort zones and build up their creativity, you need to allow irrelevant and divergent information to flow so that you will have an environment that will generate new ideas. Another interesting feature is that when you travel outside of the box, the generation of ideas happens quite fast.

For instance, you want to organize a workshop, and let us generate new ideas about how to organize a successful workshop. That is our area of focus. What is needed to organize a workshop? You need learned speakers to come for the occasion. You need an excellent theme. You need grand settings and locations. The list goes on. The idea is nothing new. I am still thinking within the box. Now I start to travel out of the box while applying a divergent modifier (to exaggerate). Instead of holding the workshop in a conference room, let us hold it in an outdoor setting in a scenic location, e.g., in a park in lovely weather. While it may have some drawbacks, such as arranging its logistics, etc., the creativity element goes up manifold when the same workshop is organized in an outdoor setting, particularly in a scenic park. From that, you get the idea. Good or bad idea, we leave it to you to assess.

Let us examine yet another example of thinking outside of the box, in terms of organizing a workshop. The core element of a memorable workshop could be its good speakers. For a moment, let's eliminate the good from the speakers and just have the speakers who may read out the scripts or the talks of well-known speakers. That way, there could be an exchange of speakers. Or there could be duets on stage instead of a single speaker. That way, we could eliminate the element of ego. These are just examples to show that it is quite possible and not too hard to think outside of the box.

Here we come to the end of this chapter. In the next chapter, we will talk about how goals should be set after due diligence.

Actionable Takeaways

Become a big-picture thinker by getting out of the box and generating creative ideas

There are times when you are at a loss to perform seemingly easy tasks. When they become hard to carry out, you need to plan and prepare. You will succeed with flying colors if you provide creative and innovative ideas while dreaming big.

Let's start with the first thing first. Why think big?

Think beyond our routine and think of something unique. The box is an imaginary limit between what we know so far and what we have not given a thought to. It is not a luxury to step out. It is a basic necessity for all thinking human beings. It is a necessity to step out of our known limits and generate new and evolving ideas to earn our dignity as thinking human beings.

But when it comes to building up and protecting our dignity, we must venture out of this box. While venturing out of the box, we can use the association of ideas, a combination of ideas, extraction of principles, and application of these principles to areas and concepts where they have never been validated before.

What conditions are conducive to thinking big?

It is generally felt that the conditions that are most favorable for men to think outside of the box are those in which men are encouraged to think creatively. When people are assured that while their creative ideas may or may not work, they will not be penalized or reprimanded for committing mistakes involuntarily. They are the only people who are encouraged to come out of their comfort zones and begin to think outside of the box. If you want to kindle and inspire people to come out of their comfort zones and build up their creativity, you need to allow irrelevant and divergent information to flow so that you will have an environment that will generate new ideas. Another interesting feature is that when you travel outside of the box, the generation of ideas happens quite fast.

CHAPTER 4:
SETTING GOALS AFTER DUE DILIGENCE

"Progress is made one step at a time. A house is built one brick at a time. Football games are won a play at a time... Every big accomplishment is a series of little accomplishments." — David J Shwartz

Many years ago, a poor landless peasant lived in a remote village in the eastern part of India with his daughter. He owed a huge debt to an old and ugly moneylender. The moneylender had an eye on the poor man's beautiful daughter. One day, he came to the poor man's house and told him that as a benevolent man he wanted to write off his debt to him, but on one condition - his daughter had to pick up a pebble from a bag. There would be only two pebbles in the bag, one black and the other white. If she took out the white one, the moneylender would waive off the entire loan, he said. If, however, she picked the black color pebble, she would have to marry the moneylender. In that event, the moneylender would also forgo the loan. The girl noticed that while picking the pebbles, the money lender picked up two black pebbles. What options did she have? Should she resign to her faith and pick the black pebble or she should expose the moneylender's evil deed at the risk of his father being harassed by the moneylender in the future?

Both of the options did not offer a tangible solution to her. Indulging in some quick thinking, while taking out the pebble from the bag, the girl dropped the pebble on the ground. "Oh, how clumsy of me," she exclaimed. "Anyway, look at the color of the pebble in the bag, if it's black, then I must have picked a white one," she said.

Having caught the moneylender in his own game, he had no choice but to waive off the entire loan to the peasant to save face. As the pebble that remained in the bag was a black one, everyone present there assumed the girl had picked the white one. And since the moneylender dared not admit his cheating, the girl managed to alter what seemed an impossible situation into an extremely advantageous one in her favor.

THE MORAL OF THE STORY:

If we give it a try, most complex problems do have a solution. We just have to think hard enough. We should try to solve the problem instead of surrendering to the situation and just giving up.

As the story illustrates, a solution that works for you may be very few. Well-defined workable plans to implement the big picture ideas are only a few. So before you get into executing one of those big ideas of yours, take a close and pragmatic look at what it will mean to you once you latch yourself on to this big idea. Examine closely all the workable tools, techniques, and resources available to you before you embark on spending your time, effort, and money on it. It may require more hard work and dedication than you originally thought. If you are ready to accept such a challenge with ease, you are ready to go.

At the start, when we initially begin to work on our big ideas, the enormity of it sometimes hits us in our face, making us act less. We are at loss to understand what we need to do now and later and in what order and progression. Hence we have to be practical and reasonable when we think big. We also have to think right at the same time.

Take one small step at a time

Break down your final goal into actionable small tasks that can be completed on a day-to-day basis. Also, allot some targets to be completed on a weekly or monthly basis. Keep checking and see how much progress you have made. As explained earlier, it is a good idea to reward yourself upon attaining a vital milestone in your journey to your final goal.

When you are working on a big-ticket goal, it is a good idea to fine-tune your vision statement as best as you can. Make yourself clear about what you want to achieve ultimately. Also, focus on your speciality segment that is especially targeted. Having a clear understanding of the micro area will give you better returns. Giving the topmost precedence and preference to the attainment of your goal will give better results, instead of all things being given the first choice which is like having no choice at all. Have a small diary or even a digital calendar on your mobile or Laptop/PC for a to-do list of the three most vital things to be completed for the day. Start by breaking these three tasks into doable segments such as within half an hour, or at the most, an hour.

Explore new frontiers of Big Thinking

Due to technological improvement in every sphere, the frontiers of thinking bigger and bigger have expanded beyond imagination. What was humanly impossible yesterday has come under the ambit of possibility. That has increased the potential of humankind many times. It has made the imagination of humankind reach new frontiers. Due to this, the self-imposed mental barriers have been broken and solutions to many of the problems are well within the reach. But the recipe for success is when we have the right ingredients.

Come out of self-notified comfort level

Leave behind the cocoon of the self-demarcated comfort zone that you have created for yourself. Experience the discomfort level as you step up your efforts to make it big while thinking big. Do not let the fear of failure and self-imposed doubts overwhelm you. As Michael Hyatt says, "There's a fine line between your discomfort zone and delusional zone. Goals in the discomfort zone challenge. Goals in the delusional zone just discourage".

Or lets us take the case of Tyler Cohen, a San Francisco-based techie who started applying for his dream job at Tech Giant, Google, in August 2019. He did not give up applying for it, even after his 39th rejection from the company, until he finally succeeded in bagging one in July 2022, when he applied for the 40th time.

"There is a fine line between perseverance and insanity. I am still trying to figure out which one I have," he says. 39 rejections and 1 acceptance, Tyler says in his short LinkedIn post, that has since gone viral. Big goals often call for persistence, which normally pays in the long run.

"Patience, persistence, and perspiration make an unbeatable combination for success," says Napoleon Hill.

Thinking big also calls for thinking right, of fully understanding that the process of achieving big success is through practical means only, not through the prism of unreasonable ability.

Revaluate your strategy, adapt to change as you fail forward

When you move up the ladder of success, there are times when you may misjudge your step and come down a couple of steps or in the worst case may fall completely. In such a scenario, weighing the options, and evaluating or changing your strategy may bring in better results. Thinking Big and not re-evaluating the progress as we move ahead may lead to wishful thinking. Repeating the same mistakes over and over and not drawing any lessons, not taking course correction measures, and hoping that one day our efforts may bring in desired goals, is nothing but wishful thinking. Remember, our wishes are not horses, and the empty daydreamers cannot ride over them.

As Stephen R. Covey said in his book, The 7 Habits of Highly Effective People, "If the ladder is not leaning against the right wall, every step we take just gets us to the wrong place faster". Hence, it is pertinent to know, while we think big, when is the right moment to take a pause and give a thought about our strategy for achieving big-ticket goals. Even questioning and assessing the quality and size of the ladder will enable us to make our journey towards the attainment of success, trouble-free.

Visualize and assess your assets

The process of thinking big involves taking one small step at a time. Chart out the course of action for completing that single step and assess and revalidate the success or the failure at certain intervals. Assess your advancement as you move along, be receptive to all the responses, recognize the points of weakness, make all the changes that may be required, and quickly check mistakes by being open to any revision. This will allow us to further polish and sharpen your strategy as you go towards the goal.

Visualizing the big picture without having a step-by-step plan to make it through may boomerang upon us. Says Cal Newport, "Great work doesn't just require great courage, but also skills of great (and real) value." These rare and valuable skills he defines as career capital. It is therefore worthwhile to equip ourselves with financial and skill capital before we embark upon our Big Picture journey. There is no point in taking the big-picture plunge before equipping ourselves with these two necessities. Acquiring these basic capitals before undertaking upon actualization of our vision is a step in the right direction.

Implementing the Big Picture

While we embark upon completing our big-picture journey, we remain open to course correction and implementation of new ideas and strategies, however small they may be, as we learn from our day-to-day progress or failures. The actualization of our goals begins with its visualization and then maintaining the right directional course followed by reassessing and revalidating our path regularly.

Let's explore how thinking big looks in action:

Whys and what of our Big Picture

Let's define "why" as representing our goal and "what" as steps that can be taken to reach the identified goal. Know you're "why" fully well. It will help you overcome any hurdle that you may come across on your way to the realization of your goal. It will also serve as a beacon of light so that you do not deviate from the chosen path. Keep reminding yourself what you wish for and why you wish. After having understood fully your "why", it will be a lot easier for "what" will naturally align itself with "why".

Taking the first baby step

Taking the first step should not be daunting. As Lao Tzu said, "The journey of a thousand miles begins with a single step". It may not be possible to plan out all your steps well in advance. You may not be aware of what the future has in store for you. But the first step is vital. And a series of steps taken in the right direction will lead us to our desired goal. Hence by putting back all the worries and procrastination behind, you will get to see the results, the fruit of your labor, however small or intangible.

Starting small is ok. What is even better is to keep assessing the situation as it emerges as you go along and not shying away from modifying the plan as the situation may demand. Delaying and putting off the initial start should at best be avoided. Identify the big picture that you want to achieve and plan out the first few steps that are best suited and take the plunge.

Paul Graham says, "The way to do really big things seems to be to start with deceptively small things".

High thinking and doing practically little to achieve it will get us nowhere. At the end of the day, what you do and how you do it and what have you achieved, matter more than what you intend to do. It is the results and not the words that are the actual stuff.

Have an undivided focus on your goal

Follow the voice of your inner conscience. Keep doing what is required to achieve your goal, even if your mind wanders and wavers at times. There are always distractions, or when you feel nobody is watching, you can take a break. As you progress, one step at a time, you will notice the compounding payback of having taken the necessary steps.

You may also see the magical effect of planning a couple of things for the day as you begin your day. This will ensure you stay focused and move towards your desired goal.

Mindset more that intellect matters

It is your mindset that matters more than your intellect and aptitude. Those having the required mindset try to put all they have learned in their life to practical use. They try to garner the latest and unique information and think of ways and means of putting them to their advantage. They try and enlarge their spear of proficiency. They attempt to put to use whatever level of knowledge level they may have. The ones who have arrived in life may not be super intelligent people but they are the ones who constantly connect with life positively.

Course adjustment

(a) Go beyond daydreaming - toil hard to make it happen

Thinking big is not just about daydreaming or just building castles in the air. Dreaming and only dreaming is not going to take us anywhere. You do not succeed just by having a wonderful vision alone. Especially when you are determined to achieve your cherished goal. It calls for solid action. It calls for a concentrated action on your part every day, in every way to make that happen. It calls for a great amount of sacrifice, audacity, self-discipline, and call for action.

Thomas Edison once said: "There is no substitute for hard work".

You have to toil really hard, and make extra effort to ensure it happens. It is not so much about "daring to think" as it is about making it happen. There would be times when you will want to give up, as your all-out efforts do not appear to bring in desired results. You will have to immune yourself from the innumerable excuses you would want to extend yourself in order to give up. The road to the realization of our life's goal would appear seemingly not possible to achieve. There are always uncountable interruptions coming your way from treading further on the chosen path. There will be risks that will detract us away. There will be failures to deter us from going further. The road to achieving success is lonely and fraught with countless hours of toil and practice, and lost sleep. There will be times when you are alone in providing yourself with much-needed support consolation and advice. As the road to the realization of our dreams is lonely, not everybody can travel along to reach their destination. The finishing line may see only a handful of people although there would have been scores of enthusiastic people at the starting line.

Those who make it to the finishing line are those who sacrificed, toiled hard, and continued despite hardships and difficulties and when giving up seemed the only tangible solution. They made it to the finishing line as they had a clear road map to achieve their goals and actively worked along and made steady progress ultimately turning their dreams into reality. All those who began at the starting point thought about making it big. But what most lacked was their inability to work really hard at it.

Hence, we begin making it happen by first hooking on to a high-flying bird to first propel us to the top of the mountain. Once we reach our cherished goal, we have to ignite ourselves with the energy to start to think of what the future holds for us in its minute details. We have then set ourselves on the road to the realization of our life's goal.

(b) Big Dreams are to be given due reverence and respect

Simply dreaming big can expose you. It can show your real worth.

Hence do not meddle with them at the cost of showing your weakness, your insecurities, or your limitations. Those who are unprepared for such exposure can witness devastating outcomes from such encounters with big dreams. Hence, learn not to be casual with your "thinking big process". It is even good to be at times fearful of them. Hence, at the starting line of "thinking big", it is good to have mixed emotions of enthusiasm, hopefulness, and conviction, along with feelings of modesty, humbleness, and anxiety. If your gut feeling tells you that you may not make it to the finishing line, do not simply take off. Give yourself more time to be ready, to prepare yourself fully. There may not be enough time for you to take a breather once you shoot off from the start line, so make sure you are ready to set off.

Here is a reality check for you. See if you are anyway willing and prepared to give up or curtail drastically all your fruitless time being spent on your mobile phone or on browsing social media activities and on various digital or electronic media platforms. If you feel you are not yet prepared for it, maybe you should give yourself some more time before taking off. But if you are aware of all the difficulties that can come your way while meeting your goal and you are willing to meet all those challenges, you, apparently, are ready to bite the dust.

In conclusion, we can safely say that while choosing your goals be vigilant. Be brutally sensible in picking up your goal ask yourself repeatedly if you have prepared well and are ready for it and are also aware of the scenario you are going to face once you have begun your journey. Have firm faith in yourself, but do not let a fantasy of an all too rosy scenario make you incapable of completing the journey.

Big thinking or big goals are achievable. If you are willing to invest your hard work and time, and are willing to give up on all those things that may make you soft, then you are in the know of what to expect and are ready to take the plunge.

As we come to the end of this chapter, in the next chapter, we will learn about certain essential elements that drive the big thinking process.

Actionable Takeaways

(1) Take one small step at a time

Break down your final goal into actionable small tasks that can be completed on a day-to-day basis. Also, allocate some targets to be completed on a weekly or monthly basis. Keep checking to see how much progress you have made. As explained earlier, it is a good idea to reward yourself upon attaining a vital milestone in your journey to your final goal.

(2) Explore new frontiers of Big Thinking

Due to technological improvements in every sphere, the frontiers of thinking have expanded beyond imagination. What was humanly impossible yesterday has come under the ambit of possibility. That has increased the potential of humankind many times.

(3) Come out of your self-notified comfort level

Leave behind the cocoon of a self-demarcated comfort zone that you have created for yourself. Experience the discomfort level as you step up your efforts to make it big while thinking big. Do not let the fear of failure and self-imposed doubts overwhelm you.

(4) Revaluate your strategy and adapt as you fail

When you move up the ladder of success, there are times when you may misjudge your step and come down a couple of steps, or in the worst case, may fall completely. In such a scenario, weighing the options, and evaluating or changing your strategy may bring better results.

(5) Visualize and assess your assets

The process of thinking big involves taking one small step at a time. Chart out the course of action for completing that single step and assess and revalidate the success or the failure at certain intervals. Assess your advancement as you move along, be receptive to all the responses, recognize the points of weakness, make all the rebalancing and changes that may be required, and quickly check mistakes by being open to any revision. This will allow you to further polish and sharpen your strategy as you go along towards the goal.

(6) Implementing the Big Picture

While we embark upon completing our big-picture journey, we remain open to course correction and implementation of new ideas and strategies, however small they may be, as we learn from our day-to-day progress or failures.

(7) Whys and what's of our Big Picture

Let us define "why" as representing our goal and "what" as the steps to be taken to achieve the identified goal. It will help you overcome any hurdle that you may come across on your way to the realization of your goal. It will also serve as a beacon light so that you do not deviate from the chosen path. Keep reminding yourself what you wish for and why you wish it.

(8) Taking the first baby step

Taking the first step should not be daunting. As Lao Tzu said, "The journey of a thousand miles begins with a single step." It may not be possible to plan out all your steps well in advance. You may not be aware of what the future has in store for you. But the first step is vital. And a series of steps taken in the right direction will lead us to our desired goal. Hence, by putting all the worries and procrastination behind, you will get to see the results, the fruits of your labor, however small or intangible.

(9) Have an Undivided Focus on Your Goal.

Follow the voice of your inner conscience and keep doing daily what is required of you to achieve your goal, even if your mind wanders and wavers at times, or there are some distractions, or when you feel nobody is watching and you can take a break. As you move along one step at a time, initially, and then as you move along with a drive, zeal and extra energy, you will see the compounding payback of having moved along the required path.

(10) Mindset more that intellect matters

It is your mindset that matters more than your intellect and aptitude. Those having the required mindset try to put all they have learned in their life to practical use. They try to garner the latest and unique information and think of ways and means of putting it to their advantage. They try and enlarge their spear of proficiency.

(11) Go beyond daydreaming - toil hard to make it happen

Thinking big is not just about daydreaming or just building castles in the thin air. Dreaming and dreaming alone is not going to take us anywhere. You do not succeed just by having a wonderful vision. Especially when you are determined to achieve your cherished goal. It calls for solid action. It takes concentrated action on your part every day in every way to make that happen. It calls for a great amount of sacrifice, audacity, self-discipline, and calls for action.

(12) Big dreams are to be given due reverence and respect

Simply dreaming big can expose you. It can show your real worth. Hence, do not meddle with them at the cost of showing your weakness, all your insecurities, and limitations. Those who are unprepared for such exposure can witness devastating outcomes from such encounters with big dreams. Hence learn not to be casual with your "thinking big process".

CHAPTER 5:
THE ESSENTIAL KEYS TO DRIVE
THE BIG THINKING PROCESS

"Start small, think big. Don't worry about too many things at once. Take a handful of simple things to begin with, and then progress to more complex ones. Think about not just tomorrow, but the future. Put a ding in the universe." — Steve Jobs

Right from our learning stages right up to our adulthood, we are often introduced to two sets of qualities, i.e., winning and losing. We are constantly reminded of the great divide that exists between these two sets of qualities. We are always reminded that "x" has made it to a particular field, be it academic or sports, business or politics. We often scream at top of our voices to show how a person has failed when they fail to cross the dividing line between success and failure. Winning and losing, however, is a matter of perception. One person's failure can be another person's step towards success or a goal. Those who are consistent winners are those who do not achieve success by luck or by destiny. Such people show the willpower to succeed as they enter into a challenge or competition, or simply when meeting day-to-day life's struggles.

However, you should incorporate the qualities that drive the process of thinking big early in life. Right from the beginning of your early life, you don't lose anything by trying to be an achiever in areas that you attempt. Let's take a look at such qualities one by one.

a) Achievers and big thinkers jump into the sport regardless of being given a formal invitation

People who wait at the sidelines to be called rarely end up being winners in the game. Success will come to those who merrily start participating in the game without waiting on the margins for a formal invitation, regardless of whether they have been asked or not. Winners are more focused on their consistent performance, rather than being engaged in other irrelevant or trivial issues. It is the winner's quality to walk up and offer their service and participation in adding value and worth to the game. If they are taken in, they eagerly lap up the offer and give their best shot at the game.

b) Seek out help. The universe has its own way to assist you

Do not believe that if you keep quiet, someone will read your mind and extend assistance. Those who boldly come forward and seek help from those who are knowledgeable or resourceful are sure to get assistance in times of need. If you genuinely seek out help, it is said that the entire universe has a way to facilitate you. People around you have to be aware of the target that you are trying to achieve. If they are ignorant of your struggles, they cannot help you even if they want to. Winners ask for things that they may require. This trait eases their way toward the fulfillment of their goals. The collective assistance of people around you may further drive your attempt to seek out your cherished goal. Very few competitions are won all by oneself and without the collective and cooperative efforts of others. To go further ahead, there is absolutely nothing wrong with seeking out help. However, keep in mind that there is a way of seeking out help from others. Courtesy and politeness are the hallmarks of seeking help while you graciously ask for what you desire. Remember, help may be available around the corner. All you have to do is to seek it out before it is too late. The universe has a way of assisting you with precise help at the precise moment.

c) Know your area of control and limitations

There are certain areas, such as the price of petrol, share prices, etc., that are way beyond the control of even successful people. There is absolutely no point in pushing their known limits in such areas which are simply a waste of time, energy, and money. It is best to leave such uncontrollable areas and move on and focus on areas that can be achieved simply by applying consistent resolve and hard work. Hence, it is best to know one's limitations and areas of strength. Those who are successful and think big try to affect change in a more positive manner in areas of their strength and power.

d) Channelize the positive energies of the people around you

An accomplished person and a big thinker exactly knows what their strengths are and also weaknesses. Most successful people also have the gift of leveraging the positive energies of those around them. They are also aware that a joint effort of all those around them makes a greater impact than attempting to achieve brilliance all by themselves. To make a joint effort to make a positive change, a successful person and a big thinker will ignite the minds of those around them by first recognizing their hidden talents and then inspiring them to achieve greater heights. A collective effort to gain a greater foothold on their way to success also means everyone is well encouraged and inspired to further contribute to their collective goal.

e) Accomplished people self-advocate

In a world where every successful person is trying to be heard above the din and noise of those around them, it is the best strategy to keep talking and keep drumming about one's accomplishments and achievements. The latest research has shown that all those who are accomplished constantly talk about themselves to be known and heard. All those who want to rise above the noise level, have to make themselves heard loud and clear. There is no point in simply giving away their precious time, energy, and money in remaining shy and apprehensive about speaking about themselves. Successful people are sure that whatever they are doing will make a positive influence on society and also on the people around them. They do not harbor any doubt or apprehension. While not unduly stressing their importance, they ensure that the world around them knows about their accomplishments and how they will impact the people in their lives positively.

f) The accomplished person knows how to move on from a defeat

It is not possible for all successful people and big thinkers to win all the time. There will be times when even achievers may experience loss and face adverse circumstances. However, there is no point in clinging to nightmares and bad experiences. The sooner one gets over it and moves on, it is going to be all the better. Focus on what lies ahead. Draw up lessons from the mistakes committed. Then reset the road map ahead to achieve the target with a positive mindset. This will be a better idea than simply clinging to the thoughts of despair and disappointment, wasting precious time and energy in the process.

g) Achievers and big thinkers go for the big-ticket experience

All accomplished people and big thinkers believe in pursuing big-ticket experiences, they are aware that small gains do not add up to a big win. Hence, they would stay clear of all such experiences, ventures, and schemes that are not worthy of attracting their attention. Since time on hand is in short supply, all successful people like to devote themselves to projects and assignments that will have a positive impact on them and also on the lives of those around them. They do not like to waste their time on small projects or assignments that have little or no impact on a social level. They also have a habit of doing all the routine and mundane things with little or no effort.

With this, we come to the end of this chapter. In the next chapter, we will learn about the factors of thinking big that **drive success.**

Actionable Takeaways

(1) Achievers and big thinkers jump into the sport regardless of being given a formal invitation

People who wait at the sidelines to be called rarely end up being winners in the game. Success will come to those who merrily start participating in the game without waiting on the sidelines for an invitation. Winners are more focused on their consistent performance rather than being engaged in other irrelevant issues.

(2) Seek out help and the universe has a way of assisting you

Do not believe that if you keep quiet, someone will read your mind and extend assistance. Those who boldly come forward and seek help from those who are knowledgeable or resourceful are sure to get assistance in times of need. If you genuinely seek out help, it is said that the entire universe has a way to facilitate you. People around you have to be aware of the target that you are trying to achieve. If they are ignorant of your struggles, they cannot help you even if they want to. Winners invariably ask for things that they may require. This trait eases their way toward the fulfillment of their goals.

(3) Know your area of control and limitations

There are certain areas, such as the price of petrol, share prices, etc., that are way beyond the control of even successful people. There is absolutely no point in pushing your limits in such areas which are simply a waste of time, energy, and money. It is best to leave such uncontrollable areas and move on and focus on areas that can be achieved simply by applying consistent resolve and hard work.

(4) Accomplished people self-advocate

In a world where every successful person is trying to be heard above the din and noise of those around them, it is the best strategy to keep talking and keep drumming about one's accomplishments and achievements.

(5) Channel positive energy from people around you

Those who are accomplished and big thinkers know exactly what their strengths and weaknesses are. Most successful people also have the gift of gab in leveraging the positive energies of those around them. They are also aware that a joint effort of all those around them makes a greater impact than attempting to achieve brilliance all by themselves.

(6) The accomplished person knows how to move on from a defeat

It is not possible for all successful people and big thinkers to win all the time. There will be times when even achievers may experience loss and face adverse circumstances. However, there is no point in clinging to nightmares and bad experiences. The sooner one gets over it and moves on, it's going to be all the better.

(7) Achievers and big thinkers go for the big-ticket experience

All accomplished people and big thinkers believe in pursuing big-ticket experiences as they are aware that small gains do not add up to a big win. Hence, they would stay clear of such experiences, ventures, and schemes that are not worthy of attracting their attention. Since time on hand is in short supply, all successful people like to devote themselves to projects and assignments that will have a positive impact on them and also on the lives of those around them.

CHAPTER 6:
HOW CAN BIG THINKING HELP YOU SUCCEED?

"You are what you think. So just think big, believe big, act big, work big, give big, forgive big, laugh big, love big and live big." — *Andrew Carnegie*

Thinking BIG seems like a natural next step when you've got big ambitions and ideas. It can be an exciting time where your mind is bursting with new possibilities, but it's also a bit of a double-edged sword. If you're thinking big, there will be more at stake—more risk and more reward. That's because with any big idea comes a lot of hard work, sleepless nights, and dedication to see it through to the end. Thinking BIG means that you are ready to put in the necessary work to make your dreams come true. But before you set out on this crazy journey, there are some things you need to know first.

(a) Knowing the latest trends is key to your success

Before you start investing time, energy, and money into making your big idea happen, you need to know if the timing is right. Making a big investment when the timing isn't right could turn a great idea into a massive failure, which will leave you feeling defeated and ready to throw in the towel. You must determine whether there is sufficient demand for your product, whether the market is prepared for it, who your target market is, and how you will reach them. If you think you have a product that people want and need but aren't sure if the timing is right, look at the latest trends. Trends are a good indication of what is popular at the moment and can clue you about what your target audience may be interested in next.

(b)Define your "why" before you dive in

The first thing you must do is define your big ideas from the beginning to plan how they will look. Why do you want to make this big idea happen? What is the purpose of your big idea? Why are you investing all of your time, energy, and money into making this a reality? These are all vital questions that need to be answered before you start making plans. You need to be 100% committed to your idea and have a strong reason as to why it's vital to you. If you don't have a strong reason as to why you want to make your big idea happen, you're likely to give up when things get tough.

(c)Stay flexible with your idea, but be firm on your vision

Having a solid idea for your big idea is vital, but you also need to remain flexible. You need to be open to change, willing to accept feedback, and ready to adapt to what the world has to offer. You never know who might end up being a great partner or customer, or even have an idea or opportunity that can take your success further. The best way is to stay flexible with your ideas while still staying firm with your resolve and vision. Having a vision board is another way to remain focused. A vision board is a great way to get your ideas and thoughts out of your head and onto paper. You can use images and words to visually map out your big idea and what you want it to look like. Making your vision board will also give you a great platform to get feedback from others and see what they think.

(d)Ask yourself some tough questions before you start making big changes

There are a lot of things that you need to consider before you continue down the path of making your big idea happen. These will be some tough questions to think about and answer for yourself before moving forward. This will be a great way for you to make sure you're ready for the challenge, and that you're putting yourself in the best position to succeed. These questions are also helpful when you need to sell your idea to others, or even when you need to explain your vision to yourself.

(e)Be an expert at the art of selling

The last thing to remember when thinking BIG is to be an expert at the art of selling. Selling is such a vital part of running any business and making your idea a reality. You need to learn to be comfortable with selling, be able to sell your idea to others, and be able to sell your product or service to your customers or clients. Your sales pitch and ability to sell your idea will determine how successful your business becomes. You can have the greatest product or service in the world, but if you can't sell it to your customers, it won't make a dime. That's why you need to make sure that you're prepared and ready to sell your product or service to anyone willing to hear your pitch.

(f) Don't forget the importance of marketing and advertising when thinking BIG

Marketing and advertising will be your best friends when it comes to making your big idea a reality. Marketing and advertising are your hands-on, tangible ways of reaching your target audience. You have to reach out to your customers and clients to make your big idea a reality. The best way to do that is to make your product visible to the world. Make sure that you are taking advantage of marketing and advertising channels such as social media, blogs, and podcasts. These are great ways to build your audience and get your product in front of as many people as possible.

Now that you know more about the things you need to know before you think BIG, you can start your journey to making your big idea a reality. There are many ways to make your big idea a reality, but the best way is to make it happen with a plan and set of goals. Set your goals and then break them down into smaller, reachable targets that you can work towards every day. Last but not least is marketing and advertising. You can't sell your idea to others if no one knows about it! Make sure to create a vision board, a business plan, and a financial roadmap that will help you take your vision from zero to one. This brings us to the close of this chapter. In the next and last chapter, we will discuss the limitless possibilities of the thinking big process.

Actionable Takeaways

(1) Knowing the latest trends is key to your success

Before you start investing time, energy, and money into making your big idea happen, you need to know if the timing is right. Making a big investment when the timing isn't right could turn a great idea into a massive failure, which will leave you feeling defeated and ready to throw in the towel.

(2) Define your why before you dive in

The first thing you must do is define your big idea's why before beginning to plan how it will look. Why do you want to make this big idea happen? What is the purpose of your big idea? Why are you investing all of your time, energy, and money into making this a reality? These are all vital questions that need to be answered before you start making plans.

(3) Stay flexible with your idea, but be firm on your vision

Having a solid idea for your big idea is vital, but you also need to remain flexible. You need to be open to change, willing to accept feedback, and ready to adapt to what the world has to offer. You never know who might end up being a great partner or customer, or even have an idea or opportunity that can take your success further.

(4) Ask yourself some tough questions before you start making big changes

There are a lot of things that you need to consider before you continue down the path of making your big idea happen. Ask yourself some tough questions to think about and answer them yourself before moving forward. This will be a great way for you to make sure you're ready for the challenge and that you're putting yourself in the best position to succeed.

(5) Don't forget the importance of marketing and advertising when thinking BIG

Marketing and advertising will be your best friends when it comes to making your big idea a reality. Marketing and advertising are your hands-on, tangible ways of reaching your target audience. You have to reach out to your customers and clients to make your big idea a reality.

CHAPTER 7:
THE " SKY IS THE LIMIT"
FOR BIG PICTURE THINKERS

"Shoot for the moon. Even if you miss, you'll land among the stars."
— *Norman Vincent Peale*

One of the vital ingredients of tasting victory or accomplishment is commitment and perseverance towards the chosen task. Other than perseverance, the next most vital element for attaining our cherished goal is how we think about the entire progression. An affirmative assessment goes a long way in making things a lot easier on the path to progress. The more positivity we bring into the way we think about achieving our goal, the more straightforward it gets in our journey toward greatness. What the future holds for us is quite uncertain. But we at least can make a sincere attempt in building it. By our continued zeal and relentless efforts and by daring to dream big, we can even turn it into reality. Success after all is nothing but the follower of those who do not wait for an opportunity but those who create it.

(a) Understanding the influence of thinking big

If we are to see the common thread between achievement, prosperity, and power, we will notice that those who got all of these had applied the belief of having big ideas early in their life. Due to this, they have managed to live a life of their imaginings as it has given them unfettered fiscal control.

(b) Be inspired daily

Our vision can be realized by acting positively daily. Little but uncomplicated changes on your end can have a significant effect on your accomplishment. First begin by drawing out one day or tiny tasks at a time while moving on towards your goal and commit to completing them daily, whether it is as simple as calling someone on a mobile phone or as complex as launching a new endorsement or creating fresh merchandise. Regardless of the size of the project, taking fast action regularly can help you get to the ultimate objective.

(c) Benefit from your confidence

The capacity to imagine huge and achieve the objective is strongly influenced by attitude. Don't constantly criticize or whine. Have a constructive approach. Keep in mind observations of people that keep you in high spirits. Every day, write down successful outcomes in your diary. Watch how you change once you begin keeping a daily journal of happy moments. You might notice accelerated development and multiplied success. You could easily upgrade your business by changing your behaviors and perspectives. So encourage positive, expansive thinking to raise your mental state. Write down successful and happy outcomes in your journal. Watch how you change once you begin keeping a daily diary of happy moments. You may notice accelerated development and multiplied accomplishments that will help you easily advance your business or your work life.

(d) Accomplishment and high thinking are linked

Those who have more money may not be more intelligent than you. You may even be giving your full potential in their comparison. The question of why they have achieved famed success and not you arises.

They differ from us in that they think differently. Their success is a result of their five times larger thought processes. We are a lot more than we are aware of being. The majority of the thoughts that we think and the thoughts that surround us are small. And precisely, that is what makes a difference.

(e) Toppers' secret

Those who have success have one common goal that aided them at every moment in their life and that yearned for. They aspired to arrive at the pinnacle even if it meant being the follower and not the one to guide from the front. Accomplishment is not directly related to circumstances, aptitude, or ability. It is a picking, an option. Do not bother about negative observations and statements made about you, belittling your capacity to achieve success. You have unconsciously stored in your brain truly believing them as you grew up. These unflattering comments may even have been made by people who are near and dear ones. However, they may not have a correct assessment of your abilities.

The wonders of thinking big are unfathomable. We have to widen our canvas of thinking. As we think so shall we become. This is completely our choice. We have to ultimately decide whether to limit our thinking thereby limiting our growth or think in abundance and grow in abundance.

(f) The prudent direction of achievement

Achievers move ahead while attempting to make their dreams a certainty. But first thing first. Move out of your comfort zone and make something happen that you always wanted to do, but were happy believing you couldn't achieve. Even if it's a small step, it is a step in the right direction. Even by achieving a small target, feel the joy of being able to do a thing all by yourself and also feel the happiness of doing what you always wanted to do. In this way, you are according to your importance and independence. A growth in your stature as you succeed in your attempts.

(g) Have total faith in yourself

It is prudent to understand that thinking big does not mean only desiring. It means placing complete trust in ourselves and our beliefs. The belief that we trust ourselves is enough to make wonders. We do not have to be extra intelligent or extra sharp. What we need is the belief that we are the finest and have to perform accordingly. That is the magic of self-assurance.

(e) Apply your secret dream from "me to we" to make it a reality

We all have a secret dream with ourselves. But according to a study, only 8% of the people who have them actually make it a reality. This 8% of the people are those who apply their dreams from "me to we". Let's take the example of Malala Yousafzai, who received a Nobel Prize at the age of 15 years. She dreamed of an education for all the children of Afghanistan. It shows that when the purpose of your dream is wide when you can apply it from "me to we", you can overcome any hurdle and can convert it into reality.

To be successful in achieving our goals, be they personal or business, and to be able to overcome difficulties in achieving them, try to shift the focus from "me to we", and see the results. Soon you will be able to get into the company of 8% of those people who are successful in completing their goals.

(f) Justification - the reason for the crash

Tony Robbins, a well-known author, says it is not due to a lack of resources that people fail. It is due to lack of resourcefulness that leads to unfulfilled dreams, or the dreams not turning into reality. Some people make various justifications for not achieving their goals. e.g. lack of education, family support, financial crunch, not having age on our side (either too young or too old), not being too healthy, or simply not having good fortune on our side are some common excuses dished out by people for not

completing their goals. We have the habit of classifying our failures with some so-called resource crunch such as age, education, financial stability, etc. We believe this lack of resources has kept us back from fulfilling of dream goals. Achievement of a goal is not dependent on some divine fortune. When we are hit by such thoughts, we have to strengthen our self-belief and be watchful of not making such excuses to justify our actions.

While we negotiate a rough patch in life, it is very easy to go back to our comfort level. However, that is the exact moment when we deny ourselves the urge to withdraw from the challenge spot and remind ourselves that we are an achiever. We should focus on those qualities, that we are sure, we possess. We should at this moment redouble our resolve to complete our goal come what may, without doubting ourselves. It is always practical to break our goal into small actionable steps. We should then learn to celebrate each completed small target, instead of comparing our performance with other competitors.

(g) Stay focused on your vision

The use of positive affirmations and verbal communication play a significant role in how we look at ourselves and also how we see people around us. As long as we are well set on our journey of daily improvement, it is quite insignificant even if we are battling with a few unsound traits. As long as we are focused on our vision, we are bound to overcome our present-day shortcomings. We should not

let our present-day inabilities make us incapable of reaching our goals. Concentrating on our positive abilities will help in overcoming whatever shortcomings we may have at present moment. Flipping away our frustration and distress is one good feature of a great person. Instead of making a comparison with others, it is more expedient to compare with the goals that we have set for ourselves. Because big rewards are achieved by taking one step at a time. However small it may be. But one step forward will lead to a series of steps and finally, we will see ourselves making progress on our journey to attaining our goals. Remember that "Only those who risk going too far will come to know how far they can go". And lastly, there is a Chinese saying that goes "A thousand-mile journey starts with a single step".

(f) Go First Class

Going First Class does not mean acquiring all the pricey things for yourself. It means associating yourself with those who have achieved success in the area that you aspire for. Keep all those negative people, who you think feel thrilled to see you tumble down, at arm's length. Stay away from all kinds of negativity and associate with like-minded achievers. After some time you will begin to see improvement in the quality of your thinking. We have to offer value to the world in whatever area we may be in before the world around us starts giving value to us in the same measure.

We have to act in the present moment. Hence start now. Do not wait for eternity, i.e. when every single factor turns in your favor for you before you start making your move. Because that will never happen. You have to act. Act right now. Now is the right moment to start getting your acts together. Outpace your acts at a more than the average speed. A speed that will outrun most of your ordinary competitors behind. So that you will be among the first to reach the finishing line.

Start your move with a strong resolve along with experimenting. The judicious mix of both along with a sprinkling of lessons learned is the sure way to go. Thinking big coupled with hard work, and determination will lead you ultimately to achieve your ambition successfully. Thinking big helps you overcome all your shortcomings, help yourself in rebuilding yourself and set you on the path of progress.

Actionable Take Away

(a) Understanding the influence of thinking big

If we are to see the common thread between achievement, prosperity, and power, we will notice that those who got all of these had applied the belief of having big ideas early in their life.

(b) Motivation is taking action daily

Dreams can be realized by taking action daily in a positive and novel manner. Small but simple changes on your end can have a significant impact on your success. First begin by drawing out small tasks towards your goal and commit to completing them daily, whether it is as simple as making a few calls every day or as complex as launching a new promotion or developing a new product.

(c) Benefit from your confidence

The ability to think big and achieve goals is strongly influenced by attitude. Don't constantly criticize or whine. Always start looking for the positive side of things. Mark posts that are supportive of your progress with praise and positive comments. Every day, write down successful outcomes in your journal. Watch how you change once you begin keeping a daily journal of happy moments.

(d) Success and big thinking are correlated

Are the people who make more money and earn better than you smarter than you? Do they put in a lot more effort than you do? If the answer is no, the question of why they have achieved famed success and not you, arises. They differ from us in that they think differently. Their success is a result of their five times larger thought processes. We are a lot more than we are aware of being.

(e) Toppers' secret

Those who earned success have one common goal that aided them at every moment in their life and that was their yearning for it. They aspired to arrive at the pinnacle even if it meant being the follower and not the one to guide from the front. Accomplishment is not directly related to circumstances, aptitude, or ability.

(f) The prudent direction of achievement

Achievers move ahead while attempting to make their dreams a certainty. But first thing first, move out of your ease zone and make something happen that you always wanted to do but were happy believing you cannot do it.

(g) Have total faith in yourself

It is prudent to understand that thinking big does not mean only desiring . It means placing complete trust in ourselves and our beliefs. The belief that we trust ourselves is enough to make wonders. We do not have to be extra intelligent or extra sharp.

(e) Apply your secret dream from "me to we" to make it a reality

We all have a secret dream with ourselves. But according to a study, only 8% of the people who have them actually make it a reality. This 8% of the people who fulfill their dreams are those who apply their dreams from "me to we".

(f) Justification - the reason for the crash

Tony Robbins, a well-known author, says it is not due to a lack of resources that people fail. It is due to lack of resourcefulness that leads to unfulfilled dreams, or the dreams not turning into reality. Some people make various justifications for not achieving their goals. e.g. lack of education, family support, financial crunch, not having age on our side, (either too young or too old), not being too healthy, or simply not having good fortune on our side are some common excuses dished out by people for not completing their goals.

(g) Stay focused on your vision

The use of positive affirmations and verbal communication play a significant role in how we look at ourselves and also how we see people around us. As long as we are well set on our journey of daily improvement, it is quite insignificant even if we are battling with a few unsound traits.

(f) Go First Class

Going First Class does not mean acquiring all the pricey things for yourself. It means associating yourself with those who have achieved success in the area that you aspire for. Keep all those negative people, who you think feel thrilled to see you tumble down, at arm's length.

CONCLUSION

When it comes to making your ideas come true, there's no one-size-fits-all. You have to think big and take risks if you want to make a real impact on the world. That's why we put together this definitive guide on how to think bigger. From your business idea to your biggest vision, we outline everything you need to get started on this essential journey.

If you want to achieve big ideas, you need to start by thinking ahead. This means taking your thoughts and ideas one step further and considering how they could be turned into a reality. By thinking about the future, you can begin to imagine what might happen and how it would impact your life. For instance, if you were interested in starting a business, you might consider thinking about what kind of products or services could be offered. Then, you could come up with a plan for marketing and advertising your product or service — making sure that your idea is heard and seen by the right people.

The first step in achieving big dreams is dreaming bigger than ever before. Most people only dream about small things — but that's okay only till the time you start exploring new territories of growth! When you start thinking about big dreams, you open up a world of possibilities for yourself. You can explore new areas of interest and creativity — which will help stimulate your mind and make goals more achievable.

In addition, dreaming larger allows you to take on greater challenges and risks because they become easier to imagine when they are much larger than anything that has come before. And finally, by becoming more creative in your dreaming practices, you increase the likelihood of achieving your goals, both large and small.

Your dream should always start with an understanding of why it matters to you — then go from there! By following these tips, any dream image can become a reality:

- Think big;
- Think forward;
- Take chances;
- Believe in yourself;
- Be creative.

One of the most vital steps in coming up with big ideas is spreading them around. You need to find people who have similar interests or goals and convince them to join forces and share yours. This can be done through social media, email lists, or even in person.

When developing a better plan, it's vital to take your ideas to the next level. This means taking them one step further and imagining how they could be executed perfectly. For example, think about ways you could make your idea more efficient or create a more effective marketing strategy. By doing this, you will help develop a better plan that can be implemented successfully.

One of the most vital aspects of thinking bigger is taking your ideas to the next level. By doing this, you can come up with concepts and plans that are even more ambitious than what you've already thought of. One way to do this is by brainstorming. When you have a lot of ideas on your mind, it can be helpful to break them down into smaller, more manageable chunks. This will help you to see how each idea could be implemented and make sure that your larger plan remains viable.

Another way to think bigger is by taking on new challenges. This means exploring new fields or areas of study that may hold some potential for success in terms of your ideas and projects. After all, if you can conquer something new, it might just inspire you to think harder about what you want to achieve in life – and maybe even take on some big challenges along the way!

In conclusion, taking your ideas to the next level and conquering new challenges are two of the most vital things you can do to make your plans come true. By following these tips, you'll be on your way to a more successful vacation plan — and maybe even a career change!

If you're thinking bigger, taking your ideas to the next level is the key to success. By spreading your ideas and taking your ideas to the next level, you'll be able to achieve great things.

As we come to the end of this book, I hope it offers some solutions for gearing up to take up the challenges of thinking big. The book has been written in a manner in which some of the ideas suggested can be interpreted and implemented as one reads through. I am sure, that if you have already implemented some of the strategies suggested for Thinking Big, you can feel a rise in your thinking abilities. Some may even want to complete the entire book before starting to implement the solutions offered in the book. In that case, you may revisit the solutions offered in the book and assess the difference in the thinking process. Though the primary aim of writing this book was to add value to the lives of my readers (i.e. you). However, I too stand to gain as I implement the recommendations of the book in my life as well. For the sake of better understanding and clarity, I have summarized some central thoughts and ideas from each chapter to provide a bird's-eye view of the content. As we all know, "we are what we repeatedly do", Aristotle said once. Let us, therefore, enrich ourselves in the abundance mindset continuously so that it takes a compound effect to leverage our creative minds and lead a meaningful and fulfilling life with abundant joy and limitless success.

While I profoundly thank you for choosing to read this book, and I also hope that the book can provide some solutions that will positively impact your thinking, can I ask you to take some moments to write a review for my book? This will help in better understanding of the book for the general readers.

Please leave your review by clicking the below link. It will directly lead you to the book review page. DIRECT REVIEW LINK FOR "HOW TO THINK 10 X". It will just take less than a minute of your time, but will tremendously help me to reach out to more people, so please leave your review.

Thanks for your support of my work.

And I'd love to see your review.

FULL BOOK SUMMARY OF "HOW TO THINK 10 X"

Chapter 1: Introduction: Key Takeaways

The Story of Jim Carrey

Chapter 2: Key Takeaways

Imagine the options

As you start to think in your mind, you might as well think big. Imagine all the good that can happen to you as you start to think big. You should not let the fear of success or failure stop you from achieving what you imagine and dream of. Imagine that the possibilities are endless.

Reading increases your perception

If you read more, you can change yourself into a big thinker. Knowledge comes by reading about it, hearing about it, and visiting the area yourself. So do not let a lack of knowledge limit you in any way. Be a voracious reader.

Widen your knowledge base by expanding your network of successful people

By expanding your network of successful people, you can also increase your knowledge base just by reading more books. When you talk to people who have made it big in their lives, your thinking prowess will be tested and will also be increased. You are further encouraged to think higher and higher by pushing the limits further.

Multiply your thinking 10 times

Thinking big requires multiplying it at least ten times. e.g., increase your career goal by ten times. The successes that you envisage in your life should be multiplied ten times. Never think small. Have big dreams. If you think big, you will reap big. It is said that if the goals that you have set for yourself do not frighten you, you are probably not setting them high enough.

Do away with all your constraints

Get rid of all your constraints and inadequacies. Stop thinking about all these restrictions that prevent you from achieving great things in life. Such thoughts act like iron chains that pull you from completing your goal.

Think from a longer perspective

Bill Gates once said: "Most people overestimate what they can do in one year and underestimate what they can do in ten years". Success is never achieved in a short time. You have to think for a long time to achieve success.

Ready to learn new aspects of life?

Try reading new books, making new acquaintances, trying out new eateries, watching new movies and watching new live dramas in theatres; experimenting with taking a new route to work or home, thinking positively, smiling often, being happy, and laughing a lot. Explore. Dream. Discover. Have complete faith in yourself. Turn that dream of yours into reality by giving everything you have got and also firmly believing and placing complete trust in your dreams.

Do it differently

When you choose your way to success, you do it by following your method instead of copying or following others. Be a leader and give 100 percent to your cherished goal. Never be scared to follow your conscience and nurture a dream.

Fail forward and fail fast

Disappointments and letdowns are part of our lives. We should accept them with open arms. They teach us vital lessons for us to take care of in the future. Hence, to achieve our end goals, we should be fully geared up to take decisions. Even if we do not succeed initially, having learned our lessons and being unmindful of our fall, we should be adaptive in our approach, stand up again and dash to our pre-set goal. Initially, you may feel uneasiness, distress, or anxiety as you topple and tumble. At first, the outcome could be disheartening. But these efforts and experiments will yield certain key learnings that will help in sharpening your skills. Gradually, your perseverance and consistent effort daily will propel you to your desired goals. You will begin to notice the improvement in results in due course. It will be largely due to your continued practice and incorporation of feedback. Hence, thinking big, coupled with experimentation, will lead to the actualization of your goals, making them a reality.

No point in listening to the cynics

It is best to listen to your inner voice when it comes to achieving your cherished goal and remain clear of all pessimists. So, listen to your inner voice every time you are in doubt.

There is no substitute for hard work

Whatever path you choose, it gives you your full potential. The lackadaisical approach does not work at all. Give everything that you have to achieve the goal you have set for yourself. Shortcuts in life do not pay off. Success does not come cheaply.

Give back to society

Give back to society by way of helping others in some form or another. The more you contribute to society at large, the more your own life will be enriched, both spiritually and materialistically, in greater measure.

The bottom line

Enthusiastically accept more challenges and opportunities. Your mind will embrace more of them as they come, as capacity is only a state of mind. Remember, top-level people do a lot more, so can you! So trust yourself.

Chapter 3: Key Takeaways

Become a Big Picture Thinker. Get out of the box and generate creative ideas

There are times when you are at a loss to perform seemingly easy tasks. When they become hard to carry out, you need planning and preparation to come out with flying colors in giving creative and innovative ideas while dreaming big.

Let's start with the first thing first. -Why think big?

Think beyond our routine and think of something unique. The box is an imaginary limit between what we know so far and what we have not given a thought to. It is not a luxury to step out. It is a basic necessity for all thinking human beings. It is a necessity to step out of our known limits and generate new and evolving ideas to earn our dignity as thinking human beings. But when it comes to building up and protecting our dignity, we must venture out of this box. While venturing out of the box, we can use the association of ideas, combinations of ideas, extraction of principles, and application of these principles to areas and concepts where they have never been validated before.

What conditions are conducive to thinking big?

It is generally felt that the conditions that are most favorable for people to think outside of the box are those who are encouraged to think creatively. When people are assured that while their creative ideas may or may not work, they will not be penalized or reprimanded for committing mistakes involuntarily, They are the only people who are encouraged to come out of their comfort zones and begin to think outside of the box. If you want to kindle and inspire people to come out of their comfort zones and build up their creativity, you need to allow irrelevant and divergent information to flow so that you will have an environment that will generate new ideas. Another interesting feature is that when you travel outside of the box, the generation of ideas happens quite fast.

Chapter 4: Key Takeaways

Take one small step at a time

Break down your final goal into actionable small tasks that can be completed on a day-to-day basis. Also, allocate some targets to be completed on a weekly or monthly basis. Keep checking to see how much progress you have made. As explained earlier, it is a good idea to reward yourself upon attaining a vital milestone in your journey to your final goal.

Explore the new frontiers of Big Thinking

Due to technological improvements in every sphere, the frontiers of thinking have expanded beyond imagination. What was humanly impossible yesterday has come under the ambit of possibility. That has increased the potential of humankind many times.

Come out of your self-notified comfort level

Leave behind the cocoon of the self-demarcated comfort zone that you have created for yourself. Experience the discomfort level as you step up your efforts to make it big while thinking big. Do not let the fear of failure and self-imposed doubts overwhelm you.

Revaluate your strategy and adapt to change as you move forward

When you move up the ladder of success, there are times when you may misjudge your step and come down a couple of steps, or in the worst case, may fall completely. In such a scenario, weighing the options and evaluating or changing your strategy may yield better results.

Visualize and assess your assets

The process of thinking big involves taking one small step at a time. Chart out the course of action for completing that single step and assess and revalidate the success or failure at certain intervals. Assess your advancement as you move along; be receptive to all the responses; recognize the points of weakness, make all the changes that may be required, and quickly check mistakes by being open to any revision. This will allow you to further polish and sharpen your strategy as you go along towards the desired goal.

Implementing the Big Picture

While we embark upon completing our big-picture journey, we remain open to course correction and implementation of new ideas and strategies, however small they may be, as we learn from our day-to-day progress or failures.

Whys and what of our big picture

Let's define "why" as representing our goal and "what" as steps to be taken to achieve it. It will help you overcome any hurdle that you may come across on your way to the realization of your goal. It will also serve as a beacon light so that you do not deviate from the chosen path. Keep reminding yourself what you wish for and why you wish it.

Taking the first baby step

Taking the first step should not be daunting. As Lao Tzu said, "The journey of a thousand miles begins with a single step". It may not be possible to plan out all your steps well in advance. You may not be aware of what the future has in store for you. But the first step is vital. And a series of steps taken in the right direction will lead us to our desired goal. Hence, by putting all the worries and procrastination behind you, you will get to see the results, the fruit of your labor, however small or intangible.

Have an undivided focus on your goal

Follow the voice of your inner conscience and keep doing what is required of you to achieve your goal daily, even if your mind wanders and wavers at times, or there are some distractions, or when you feel nobody is watching and you can take a break. As you move along one step at a time, initially, and then as you move along with a drive, you will see the compounding payback of having moved along the required path.

Mindset matters more than intellect

It is your mindset that matters more than your intellect and aptitude. Those having the required mindset try to put all they have learned in their life to practical use. They try to garner the latest and unique information and think of ways and means of putting it to their advantage. They try and enlarge their scope of proficiency.

Going beyond daydreaming - toil hard to make it happen

Thinking big is not just about daydreaming or just building castles in the air. Dreaming and only dreaming is not going to take us anywhere. You do not succeed just by having a wonderful vision alone. Especially when you are determined to achieve your cherished goal. It calls for solid action. It takes concentrated action on your part every day in every way to make that happen. It calls for a great amount of sacrifice, audacity, and self-discipline and is a call to action.

Chapter 5: Key Takeaways

Achievers and big thinkers jump into the sport regardless of being given a formal invitation

People who wait at the sidelines waiting to be called to join rarely end up being winners in the game. Success will come to those who merrily start participating in the game without waiting on the margins or the sidelines for an invitation regardless of whether they have been asked or not. Winners are more focused on their consistent performance rather than being engaged in other irrelevant or trivial issues.

Seek out help, and the universe has a way of assisting you

Do not believe that if you keep mum, someone will read your mind and extend the assistance that you may require at times. Those who boldly come forward and seek help from those who are knowledgeable or resourceful are sure of getting assistance in times of need. If you genuinely seek out help, it is said that the entire universe has a way to facilitate you. People around you have to be aware of the target that you are trying to achieve. If they are ignorant of your struggles, they cannot help you even if they want to. Winners invariably ask for things that they may require. This trait eases their way toward the fulfillment of their goals.

Know your areas of control and limitations

There are certain areas, such as the price of petrol, share prices, etc., that are way beyond the control of even successful people. There is absolutely no point in pushing their known limits in such areas, which is simply a waste of time, energy, and money. It is best to leave such uncontrollable areas and move on and focus on areas that can be achieved simply by applying consistent resolve and hard work.

Accomplished people are self-advocates

In a world where every successful person is trying to be heard above the din and noise of those around them, it is the best strategy to keep talking and keep drumming about one's accomplishments and achievements.

Channelize the positive energies of the people around you

A successful person and a big thinker are well aware of both their strengths and weaknesses. Most successful people also have the gift of gab while leveraging the positive energies of those around them. He is also aware that a joint effort of all those around him makes a greater impact than attempting to achieve brilliance all by himself

The accomplished person knows how to move on from a defeat

It is not possible for all successful people and big thinkers to win all the time. There will be times when even achievers may experience loss and face adverse circumstances. However, there is no point in clinging to nightmares and bad experiences. The sooner one gets over it and moves on, it's going to be all the better.

Achievers and big thinkers go for the big-ticket experience

All accomplished people and big thinkers believe in pursuing big-ticket experiences as they are aware that small gains do not add up to a big win. Hence, they would stay clear of all such experiences, ventures, and schemes that are not worthy of attracting their attention. Since time on hand is in short supply, all successful people like to devote themselves to projects and assignments that will have a positive impact on them and also on the lives of those around them.

Chapter 6: Key Takeaways

Knowing the latest trends is key to your success

Before you start investing time, energy, and money into making your big idea happen, you need to know if the timing is right. Making a big investment when the timing isn't right could turn a great idea into a massive failure, which will leave you feeling defeated and ready to throw in the towel.

Define your why before you dive in

The first thing you must do is define your big idea is to plan how it will look at the beginning. Why do you want to make this big idea happen? What is the purpose of your big idea? Why are you investing all of your time, energy, and money into making this a reality? These are all vital questions that need to be answered before you start making plans.

Stay flexible with your ideas, but be firm in your vision

Having a solid idea for your big idea is vital, but you also need to remain flexible. You need to be open to change, willing to accept feedback, and ready to adapt to what the world has to offer. You never know who might end up being a great partner or customer, or even have an idea or opportunity that can soar your success further.

Ask yourself some tough questions before you start making big

changes

There are a lot of things that you need to consider before you continue down the path of making your big idea happen. These will be some tough questions to think about and answer for yourself before moving forward. This will be a great way for you to make sure you're ready for the challenge, and that you're putting yourself in the best position to succeed.

Don't forget the importance of marketing and advertising when thinking BIG

Marketing and advertising will be your best friend when it comes to making your big idea a reality. Marketing and advertising are your hands-on, tangible ways of reaching your target audience. You have to reach out to your customers and clients to make your big idea a reality.

Chapter 7: Key Takeaways

Understanding the influence of thinking big

If we are to see the common thread between achievement, prosperity, and power, we will notice that those who got all of these had applied the belief of having big ideas early in their life.

Motivation is taking action daily

Dreams can be realized by taking action daily, in a positive and novel manner. Small but simple changes can have a significant impact on your success. First, begin by drawing out tiny tasks while moving on towards your goal and commit to completing them daily, whether it is as simple as making a few calls or as complex as launching a new promotion or developing a new product.

(c) Benefit from your confidence

The ability to think big and achieve goals is strongly influenced by attitude. Don't constantly criticize or whine. Always start looking for the positive side of things. Mark posts that are supportive of your progress with praise and positive comments. Every day, write down successful outcomes in your journal. Watch how you change once you begin keeping a daily journal of happy moments.

Success and big thinking are correlated

Are the people who make more money and earn better than you smarter than you? Do they put in a lot more effort than you do? If the answer is no, the question of why they have achieved renowned success and not you arises. They differ from us in that they think differently. Their success is a result of their five times larger thought processes. We are a lot more than we are aware of being.

Toppers' secret

Those who earned success have one common goal that aided them at every moment in their life and that was their yearning for it. They aspired to arrive at the pinnacle, even if it meant being the follower and not the one to guide from the front. Accomplishment is not directly related to circumstances, aptitude, or ability.

The prudent direction of achievement

Achievers move ahead while attempting to make their dreams a certainty. But first things first. Move out of your comfort zone and make something happen that you have always wanted to do but were happy believing you could not do it.

Have total faith in yourself

It is prudent to understand that thinking big does not mean only desiring. It means placing complete trust in ourselves and our beliefs. The belief that we trust ourselves is enough to do wonders. We do not have to be extra intelligent or sharp.

Apply your secret dream from "me to we" to make it a reality

We all have a secret dream about ourselves. But according to a study, only 8% of the people who have them actually make it a reality. 8% of the people who fulfill their dreams are those who apply their dreams from "me to we".

Justification: the reason for the crash

Tony Robbins, a well-known author, says it is not due to a lack of resources that people fail. It is due to lack of resourcefulness that leads to unfulfilled dreams, or the dreams not turning into reality. Some people make various justifications for not achieving their goals. Lack of education, family support, financial crunch, not having age on our side (either too young or too old), not being too healthy, or simply not having good fortune on our side are some common excuses dished out by people for not completing their goals.

Stay focused on your vision

The use of positive affirmations and verbal communication play a significant role in how we look at ourselves and also how we see people around us. As long as we are well set on our journey of daily improvement, it is quite insignificant even if we are battling with a few unsound traits.

Go First Class

Going First Class does not mean acquiring all the pricey things for yourself. It means associating yourself with those who have achieved success in the area that you aspire to. Keep all those negative people, who you think would feel thrilled to see you tumble down, at arm's length.

A PREVIEW OF MY BOOK "TEN WAYS TO MASTER PUBLIC SPEAKING AND EFFECTIVE COMMUNICATION"

Introduction

Glossophobia (uneasiness due to public oratory) is a universal fear affecting around 75% of the population. The fright of death comes next. Oratory students know that preparing for it takes much more than just having good content. At the same time, when addressing the viewers, even those who have years of experience in speech-making can feel anxious and nervous while going on stage. Due to a lack of proper scientific education on the critical topic of rhetoric and given little professional help and expert guidance, some people resort to the trial-and-error method. However, the good news is that with the help of specific tips and guidelines, speech-making can be turned from stage fright to a stage-ready experience. As Napoleon famously said, "The art of war is a science in which everything has to be calculated and thought out". It is equally valid for oratory as well. Every speech-making occasion, much like a war, is a unique event where the entire process has to be thought out with all its threadbare details and ideas. And there is no one set of arrangements, skill set, or vision that will suit all speech-making occasions. No one size fits all. However, all good orators keep an orderly account of ideas to garner the listeners' attention.

This arrangement of ideas is a common thread among all orators, making them good presenters. Although they may be speaking on different topics, an orderly presentation of ideas by the presenter makes the audience sit up and listen to him with rapt attention. It is this presentation of an idea to the audience's mind in such a manner that the listeners are curious while listening to the talk and involuntarily allow the entry of a new idea from the orator into the listener's mind. So the first step to making a great speech is to ignite the minds of the listeners by arousing their curiosity and thereby transporting the idea to them. Therefore, the audience's minds are in sync with the presenter's mind. In this step, the millions of neurons taking shape in the speaker's mind ignite the listeners' minds and take a similar condition. These neurons are nothing but the new idea that is being talked about by the speaker.

What is an idea, after all? The idea is that patterns of information come in all shapes and sizes — some are easy, and some are complex. However, if the idea is communicated correctly, it can forever change how someone thinks about the world, shaping their actions for the present and also for future generations. That is why ideas are the most powerful force shaping human culture.

In this book, I have briefly mentioned some of the main principles required to master the art of oratory. These principles have been tested in practice by the practitioners of public speaking. Some of the essential aspects of preparation and general speaking delivery are explained in this book. Using the techniques described in this book, one can systematically and confidently present one's ideas to the listeners-big or small-a process one will master over time and be a proficient public speaker.

Chapter 1

Effective Strategies and Tips For Gaining Confidence While Speaking Publicly

A) Overcome the fear of public speaking in any situation

As a child, I had stage fright whenever I was called on stage to recite poetry or a short story in front of an audience. It was primarily due to an incident when I slipped on stage while climbing up the podium stairs. The other children laughed and mocked me. I could not utter a single word as I froze on stage. It has never been the same after that day. Most people who fear public speaking have traumatic past public speaking experiences and often fear repeating them and becoming a subject of ridicule from the audience. Many people fear public speaking more than they fear death.

My own experience with public speaking was no better. I was too terrified to speak before the audience and tried to do anything to escape the ordeal of public speaking. If public speaking became inevitable, either I would start stammering before the crowd, or I would freeze without uttering a single word. While growing up as a young man, giving interviews before a handful of people or participating in group discussions also became an arduous task.

Soon, I realized that I would not be cured of this disorder by some divine providence. I knew by then that I would have to learn all the tricks of the trade and master the art of public speaking if I was ready to grab the opportunities coming my way.

Presently, I enjoy standing before the crowd and telling stories, giving impromptu speeches that are pretty appreciated, and hosting media training centers and electronic media talk shows. In one of my part-time assignments, I taught a group of fifty students the basics of communication as a guest faculty. I have also successfully faced interview boards and participated in group discussions where I have put forth my point of view convincingly.

B) The transformation

An incident that had a profound impact on my public speaking was when one of the star campaigners for the local public representative visited our community some four years ago. After his inspiring speech, he encouraged the audience to share ideas for more extensive public participation in civic matters. While I had a good idea of what I wanted to convey, I was too scared to stand up and give my opinion; I got my perspective from a friend standing beside me. Hearing my concept, he immediately went on stage and presented it before the audience - something I was too scared to do.

The star speaker, upon hearing the concept, was very happy and hugely complimented my friend. I was both angry with myself and delighted that my idea was welcomed. I was disappointed with myself and thought of finding a solution to this problem and ultimately overcoming this issue. Besides, I was getting nowhere in my interviews to secure a steady job as I could not express myself before the interview board, although I was doing well on written tests. It was that time when I decided that enough was enough, and I would do anything and everything required to conquer my fear of speaking in public.

I started reading all that came my way on public speaking and how to conquer the fear of speaking and watched all the excellent speakers on the internet. Gradually, by sheer experimentation and genuine attempts to acquire this new skill and learn what works best for me, I started observing small steps initially to prepare myself to speak my mind coherently and explicitly in front of the crowd.

C) Baby steps

Not wanting to feel belittled before my well-wishers and friends who would breeze through any public speaking event, I decided to pull up my sleeves and do well, even on those occasions where I was addressing a huge crowd.

I even took the help of a professional counselor to provide much-needed mental strength. The counselor offered some valuable tips, asking me initially not to look toward the audience while speaking. He also suggested I see what works best for me in given situations as no two people may face the same set of problems. There's no point in comparing myself to someone who doesn't have the same issue. I thought about solutions that best suited me while facing the audience. So, I dedicated myself to finding ways to take the first few steps. And one by one, I started prioritizing certain practices, which I began to pursue before every occasion when I had to speak publicly.

D) Before the day

Step 1: Get acquainted with the location

Whenever possible, I try to see the place where I have to speak the day before the actual event. I take a stroll around the venue and get to know the area, feeling the people who would be before me while I speak on the day of the event. I get a fair idea of what to expect to improve my performance.

Step 2: Writing the speech

It is better to write down the salient points of your speech by hand and not resort to typing the entire script. I would be armed with this vital piece of paper while practicing the presentation. It is generally found that writing the script by hand empowers you with greater confidence. It gives me a different kind of reassurance in knowing that I had written the speech while also noticing the errors and edits.

Recent research has shown that we process the given information more deeply if we write the matter. The confidence level builds up seeing the self-written speech with corrections and edits. Research has shown that writing things down on paper helps in more profoundly processing the information and building up self-assurance.

Step 3: Practicing before the mirror in a complete outfit

I dread facing the scenario where I am the laughing stock of the audience and disappointing them with a below-par performance. I feel unsure of my voice, I feel self-conscious about my accent, pose, gesture, and attire. In these circumstances, I have found the mirror gives the best assessment. Invariably, I finish my presentation at least two days before the appointed day, while practicing before the mirror as much as I can. The practice session before the mirror would also include two sessions with full outfits that I plan to wear on the presentation day.

These practice sessions in front of the mirror greatly assist me in looking at my poise, accent, and gestures to figure out everything from how I stand, how I smile, and how I gesticulate. These sessions also make me stress-free to quite an extent as I know what I will say, how I will smile, and how I am going to stand. That's the way I choose to remain confident, focused, and secure in my thoughts.

Step 4: Before the actual Day

Doing a mock-up presentation before friends and family members just before the actual day, whom I trust and who give their honest feedback on some of the essential elements such as where to pause, where to go for high pitch, and seek clarifications and give advice as to how to better my presentation. This technique helps me prepare for any unscripted portion of the presentation or interview.

E) On the day

Step 1: I arrive at the venue early.

By arriving early, I avoid the dreadful thought of having to address the crowd after arriving late for the speech-making event, with no preparation and getting tongue-tied at the beginning of the speech itself. I invariably arrive one to two hours early to avoid this dreadful scenario. It allows me to recollect all that I have to say mentally. And if the room or the venue is unfamiliar to me, I would walk and take a look around to get the feel of the place.

Besides, arriving early also has other pros, like getting my laptop tuned in with the projection system, which gives me additional confidence.

Additional time also gives me a window to talk to other speakers present and chit-chat with the backstage technical crew members to acquaint myself with the scene.

Step 2: Trying to stay relaxed

Just before the event is about to begin, my heart begins to palpitate. At times, even my head starts swinging around and I can't think of anything. Those speakers who are new to this are sitting beside me, and having the same edginess appears to push me further towards the hill. I try to find some space away from all this and relax by taking long, deep, and slow breaths.

Hence the last hour before my public speaking event, I try not to look at the script and limit myself to controlling my breath and keeping my nervousness in check.

Step 3: Be the first speaker, if possible

There are chances that the long wait can result in anxiety and apprehension.

If I am required to wait for my turn and listen to others' speeches, the possibilities are that I may forget what I have to say altogether due to the built-up nervousness level. While waiting for my turn, I keep my fingers crossed for an unknown outcome of my presentation, can only increase my panic level. Hence, given a possibility or a choice, I request the organizers to speak first before the others.

Speaking first helps me stay focused on what I have to say without judging myself by others' performance.

Step 4: Speak with pauses

My main worry is to avoid nervousness while speaking. At times my mouth dries up, my jaw drops, and my throat chokes up due to stage fright. If that happens, it is quite a task for me to bounce back into the speech and still make a good impression.

I take a slight pause after two and three sentences to avoid this. While this gives me a window space to recollect my thoughts while taking a deep breath, it allows the audience to understand the chain of ideas coming from me. Recent studies have shown that pauses convey a more truthful interpretation of facts, making it more genuine and hence more interesting.

I always keep a water bottle that helps me take a water break every fifteen minutes, especially when taking classes with students.

Step 5: Talking in small, precise sentences

Another method to not get too anxious is to talk in small but accurate sentences. Long sentences should be avoided at any cost. It indeed makes me forget what I was speaking about. And the audience will also lose track of what you are saying. To remain on track, lest I forget what I was talking about, I also keep a card with salient points written about my speech. It helps me stay on track with my remarks.

While presenting from a laptop, I always keep a card or a piece of paper to write down the presentation's main points. Though earlier I used to read the entire speech on paper, I have now gained confidence in keeping the main points noted on a piece of paper after steady practice.

Step 6: Not focusing on people's faces

Studies have revealed that making eye contact is an essential element that helps speech become memorable. But when I looked into people's eyes while speaking before a large crowd, I would forget my lines and begin to think about what the person in the audience was thinking of my speech. I would start to have apprehensions that they are either bored or annoyed about what I have just said. It would further trigger anxiety and nervousness. It was another factor in my fear of speaking in public.

But by some trial and error method, it soon dawned on me that if I do not look into the eyes of someone directly and, on the other hand, give the impression of looking into the faces of the audience, then it would appear that I am talking to them. While I am not staring into the audience's eyes, it gives me relief as I cannot find out their expressions.

And I keep rotating the focus of my glance back and forth into the audience without looking individually at anyone in particular.

Step 7: Preparing for Impromptu Speeches

Small family gatherings are the best occasions for making short impromptu speeches where one can practice speaking in public without fear of being in an awkward situation.

Initially, I was even scared to speak at family gatherings. However, our family gatherings are usually occasions when all youngsters are allowed to speak their minds. But again, I was petrified about what they would think about me.

However, I was encouraged to speak my mind at family gatherings because even if I choked with emotion or stammered due to fear of getting attention, I would not be too bothered as, after all, it was only a family gathering.

Step 8: Accepting my awkwardness was helpful

When I face many naughty students in a classroom while teaching, it helps me discover my shortcomings to a greater extent, I soon realize that I am not too confident when I address them. This realization has, for some time, helped me reduce my anxiety level.

Hence, I accept at the very beginning of any impromptu speech that I am not very good at being in the limelight and do not have any prior preparation. In casual gatherings, this honest acceptance has eased my nervousness to some level.

There is every possibility that the majority of those listening would not be too good at making public speeches. Hence there is a chance that the "imperfect audience" may be more forgiving and would accept me sympathetically as a speaker. Thus, the audience's fear of examining me too closely on my content and style and laughing and ridiculing me seems to have less probability.

Step 9: Making jokes at your expense will have the audience slightly more accepting

Minor mistakes do inevitably occur during long speeches. Those who are more sensitive to their criticism can hear some of the audience passing comments or a giggle, which is enough to derail your chain of thought, leading to a further increase in anxiety. An occasional joke cracked at your own expense can trigger a positive audience response. It lightens the mood in general and creates a fun atmosphere. For example, if I ever face an awkward situation in front of a room full of people before a speech, I dare to laugh it off, saying, "That was choreographed" or "I fell harder than I intended after all". Such remarks would remove any traces of humiliation in their minds while turning it into a joke and can start all over it again with a clean slate.

Step 10: Believe in what you say

If the topic is selected judiciously, half the battle is won already. If the chosen topic is close to my heart and I firmly believe in it and cherish sharing the idea with others, then the speech would be a cakewalk and trouble-free and may also stir up emotional support from the audience.

Once I was attending an inter-college debating event where the negative fallout of technology and modern culture on youth was being discussed. The organizers announced from the stage that they were looking for volunteer speakers from the audience who would speak on the given topic without any preparation.

The event was a big one, and I, mustering all the courage signed up to be one of the volunteer speakers. It was a huge event, but still, I gathered my nerves to sign up as a speaker. I went to the stage and talked about the adverse effects of social media sites as I knew someone who had suffered hugely from such networking sites. I had jotted specific points on a piece of paper and written certain figures and factual data related to the topic. I spoke for 30 minutes, which even I didn't expect. I made a mark that day and impressed the people who even gave me a prize for my speech. But above all, I was hugely happy with myself for bringing glory to myself. The credit for delivering a resounding speech mainly goes to the fact that the topic was very dear to me, and I spoke from the core of my heart, believing in every word that I spoke that day.

--End of Preview-- Get your copy of the full book by typing the link:-

https://www.manjultewari.com/books/ten-ways-to-master-public-speaking-and-effective-communication/

"Tens Ways to Master Public Speaking and Effective Speaking"

REFERENCES

-The Magic of Thinking Big: David J. Schwartz,

-Bold: How to Go Big, Create Wealth, and Impact the World by Peter H. Diamandis and Steven Kotler

-The Small Big: Small Changes That Spark Big Influence by Steve J. Martin, Noah J. Goldstein, and Robert B. Cialdini

-The Little Book of Thinking Big: Aim Higher and Go Further Than You Ever Thought Possible by Richard Newton

-Playing Big: Find Your Voice, Your Mission, Your Message by Tara Mohr

-Essentialism: The Disciplined Pursuit of Less By Greg McKeown

-You Are a Badass: How to Stop Doubting Your Greatness and Start Living an Awesome Life by Jen Sincero,

-Be Obsessed or Be Average by Grant Cardone

-Mindset: The New Psychology of Success by Carol S. Dweck,

-Abundance: The Future Is Better Than You Think by Peter H. Diamandis, Steven Kotler

BOOK BY THE SAME PUBLISHER

"India A Cultural Voyage - A Cultural Survey of the Land of Eternal Resurgence"

About the book

The book "India: A Cultural Voyage " traces the voyage of Indian Culture through its excellences in the realms of religion, philosophy, aesthetics, languages and sciences with a lively and unique system of deciphering unity in diversity.

The book focuses mainly on India's languages, religions, dance, music, architecture, food and customs that differ from place to place.

Indian Culture, considered a combination of several cultures, has been influenced by a history of several millennia old, beginning with the Indus Valley Civilization and several other older civilizations.

The book's central theme is the element of Indian Culture, such as Indian religion, languages, mathematics, philosophy, cuisine, languages, dance, music, and festivals, which also have had a profound impact across the Indian Sub Continent and the world.

This book vividly describes India's cultural strides through more than thirty centuries.

In conformity with the general design, the book contains READINGS from Kadambari, Mahabharat, Gandhi, secular saints, flora, and festivals.

India is a land of eternal resurgence. Writing history might or might not have been a vocation with ancient Indians. Creating history through a ceaseless process of an on looking culture has definitely been a divine pastime. Cultural strides in India through more than thirty centuries is the theme of this book. It provides an insight to survey linkages of those strides lauded and aspired for by the mankind. The book is an ocean encased in crystal bowl with inner appearances made to whisper in truer lights. The book traces the voyage of Indian Culture through its excellences in the realms of religion, philosophy, aesthetics. languages and sciences with a lively and unique system of deciphering unity in diversity.

Visit the link to purchase

https://www.manjultewari.com/books/india-a-cultural-voyage/

About the Author

Mr. Manjul Tewari is a Corporate Communication practitioner. He has worked as the core group member of the Corp. Comm. Team in one of the largest power companies in the world, handling many prestigious Corp. Comm. assignments. Before joining the Corp. Comm. fraternity, he worked as a journalist in leading newspapers and periodicals. Mr. Tewari has written several articles on various topics of general interest for well-known newspapers. He is a guest faculty for many Communication and Mass Media Institutes in India. Recently he has been awarded the PR Hall Of Fame Award by the Public Relations Council of India (PRCI) in a function held in Goa. Mr. Tewari is also a widely traveled person both in India and overseas.